"We hear from thousands of parents across the United States, and I know that *What Do We Say? What Do We Do?* answers parents' needs for real help about everyday worries that keep us awake at night. Parents will sleep better when they have this very special book."

—Caroll T. Miller, publisher,
www.familyeducation.com

"Across the nation, educators are seeking productive ways to help every family know how to address typical children's home/school problem situations. *What Do We Say? What Do We Do?* is an ideal basic 'text' for school discussion groups and PTAs. Positive words and actions from home can make all the difference in children's school experience . . . and achievement."

—Ronald J. Areglado, Associate
Executive Director of
Programs, the National
Association of Elementary
School Principals

"Teachers have long admired the work of Dorothy Rich and are using her parent-involvement programs extensively. I can see teachers and families finding this book wonderfully helpful."

—Don Cameron, Executive
Director, National Education
Association

"*What Do We Say? What Do We Do?* offers an excellent bibliography of children's books about problem situations that we face as children grow up and go to school. What a great way to combine literacy development and problem-solving skills for children and adults working together on their MegaSkills.®"

—Susan Roman, Ph.D., Executive
Director, Association for Library
Service to Children/American
Library Association

**Also by Dr. Dorothy Rich**

*MegaSkills: How Families Can Help Children
Succeed in School and Beyond*
*MegaSkills: The Best Gift You Can Give
Your Child*
*MegaSkills: Children's Achievement for Our Era of
Information and Change*

**Building:**

- *Confidence*

- *Motivation*

- *Effort*

- *Responsibility*

- *Initiative*

- *Perseverance*

- *Caring*

- *Teamwork*

- *Common Sense*

- *Problem Solving*

# What Do We Say?
# What Do We Do?®

## Vital Solutions
## for Children's Educational
## Success

## Dr. Dorothy Rich

**author of**
**MegaSkills®: The Best Gift You Can Give Your Child**

How Parents Get Great Results
Using MegaSkills Conversations

A Tom Doherty Associates Book
New York

A Forge Book
Published by Tom Doherty Associates, Inc.
175 Fifth Avenue
New York, NY 10010

Forge® is a registered trademark of Tom Doherty Associates, Inc.

MegaSkills® and What Do We Say? What Do We Do?® curricula
are registered trademarks of Dorothy Rich.

Library of Congress Cataloging-in-Publication Data

Rich, Dorothy.
    What do we say? What do we do? : vital solutions for
children's educational success / Dorothy Rich.
        p.    cm.
    "A Tom Doherty Associates book."
    ISBN 0-312-85433-1
    1. Education—Parent participation—United States.
    2. School children—United States—Life skills guides.
    3. Home and school—United States.    4. Success—United
States.    I. Title.
    LB1048.5.R53    1997
    371.19'2—dc21                                          97-7858
                                                              CIP

*Book design and illustrations by Judith Stagnitto Abbate*

First Edition: August 1997

Printed in the United States of America

0   9   8   7   6   5   4   3   2   1

*For All of Us Working Hard to Educate*
*Children in the Greatest of Times and Times*
*Not So Great, Doing the Best We Can . . .*
*and Even More . . .*

*To my husband, Spencer Rich, and*
*my children, Rebecca, Jessica, and Jon,*
*who have supported my work beyond measure*
*and who work hard educating me . . .*
*doing the best they can and even more . . .*

# Contents

## Problem Solving: Families Learning Together

## Growing Along with Our Children

 *Essay*

 *Situation—Younger Children*

 *Situation—Older Children*

 *Adult Connection*

 *Reading Together—Younger Children*

 *Reading Together—Older Children*

# *Preface*

## Getting Ourselves Ready
## for Our Children's School

THERE IS NO DENYING it. When our children go to school, we go to school. We may not be physically there. But, we are there, not so much in our children's classrooms of today, but in the classrooms we knew and experienced. And the joys and the heartaches of school life all come back.

Are we ready for the inevitable crises and disappointments, minor and major, that our children bring home from school? Do we know what to say and what to do? Or are we saying again what we heard when we were kids?

From what I hear from parents across the nation, we are not as ready as we would like to be. When our children come home worried and frightened, sometimes crying, it's hard on them, but it's also hard on us, too.

We want children to be prepared for school . . . but what about the preparation that adults need? To tell the truth, I had not realized, after years of teaching and writing about education, that adults need more help than we have been offering.

There has been a lot written about how to build children's abilities (my own work has focused on this topic for 25 years). It was only after the publication of the basic *MegaSkills* books focusing on children, that I began hearing more and more from parents about their own needs.

While I was providing help for children, I was inadvertently over-looking the help that the children's helpers needed, and I became determined to work on this. I began meeting with our MegaSkills® groups across the nation. "Today let's talk not just about the children . . . tell me about the help you need." The conversation started and it has not stopped.

That's the reason for this book: It is about specific support that adults say they need in order to help their children achieve. Parents are the primary teachers and coaches in children's lives. This doesn't just come naturally. It's hard, daily work, experimentation, trial and error and, yes, trying again.

*What Do We Say? What Do We Do?* differs from my other work in that it focuses on specific home-school problems and the words and actions that help us through the process of solving these problems.

Today, we often don't know that the family down the street is having the same home-school problems that we are. That's what the parents in our MegaSkills Program told me. Until they came to the workshops, they didn't know how common their own problems were. What they needed, they said, was someone to talk it over with.

That's what this book is designed to be: a talk with a friend. The situations in this book are meant to be tried on for size. They may fit exactly or they may need some alteration to fit. What they provide are rehearsals, practices for the real thing, the everyday problems that come home. Our goal is to help our children develop resiliency and competence for life today and tomorrow. Through this book, we see the everyday problems that come home from school as opportunities for teaching and learning.

Check the Table of Contents to find situations that fit your needs now or those that seem more likely to happen at your house. Try them out.

Read the chapters in any order. Read the stories of Randy and Donna or David or Angela. These are real kids with real dilemmas. They could be yours.

Use the questions and the responses presented in this book. Try to be as interactive as possible with the material. Ask yourself: How similar or different are the situations from what happens in our house? Would my child ask that or something else? Would I say that? How would I change what the parent in this book says? What happens next? How can we build on what we say and do?

Our work is never over . . . and that's the greatest challenge and the greatest hope for us all.

—DR. DOROTHY RICH

# Introduction

## Wanting the Best for
## Our Children

**A**S PARENTS OUR GREATEST hopes focus on our children and helping them realize their dreams.

Today, more than ever, realizing dreams takes education. It means that children and the grown-ups who care for them need to know how to learn. It means that our children become successful learners for life, not just in school but also beyond the classroom.

We can all agree that we want the "best" for our children. But what does the "best" mean in a rapidly changing world, where a computer up-to-date six months ago can be out-of-date six months later. There are so many choices, so many different points of view, so many cable channels and Internet addresses we can't keep count.

The experts have a lot to tell us and yet often, their opinions collide. There is no one answer, from when is the best time to toilet train to when is the best time to buy back-to-school supplies. It can get very confusing and very hard to find practical answers to: WHAT IS THE BEST FOR MY CHILD?

We read the headlines and hear the news reports. The world, even our own neighborhoods, are often dangerous places, for us and our children. Where do we go? Whose lead do we follow? Caught up in the rush of our daily lives, it can be very tempting to throw up our hands and say, "We just don't know."

And yet . . . the truth is that we really do know.

When parents across the nation are asked what is the *best* they want for their children, answers center on the cornerstones of character: responsibility, dependability, curiosity, confidence, eagerness to learn, independence, self-discipline, sensitivity to others, kindness, consideration, willingness to work hard.

It makes no difference who we are. These answers are the same for everyone, everywhere. They are the eternals and we know them. I call these MegaSkills. They are the values, attitudes, behaviors, and habits that make all the difference in life. They span the generations. They are the bedrock of our democracy, our way of life.

In the tumult of everyday life, parents can overlook these basics or assume children, who look so grown-up, and seem to know so much about the world . . . already know them or will learn them on their own. Unfortunately, this is not how it's working. The attitudes and behaviors that help us successfully through life have to be taught and learned . . . sometimes more than once.

It is hard to know how to teach the *best*. I've been told by parents and teachers that I help them teach the *best*. This really encourages me, because this is my dream, my hope. It's not enough just to talk and write about how to help children. We have to focus more on how to provide specific, practical help for the significant adults in children's lives . . . us!

## MegaSkills Conversations

When I first said the word "MegaSkills" in the middle of a presentation to a group of educators in 1987, I didn't stop to explain. Actually, I said it in a whisper. I had formulated this word in my mind to signify the really important basics that students and their families need to learn in order to succeed. I didn't know if it would mean anything to others. At the end of my talk, I heard a voice at the back of the room: "What are those *MegaSkills*?"

From that one voice has come many voices across the nation. I had articulated and defined a concept more powerful, more mobilizing of interest and energy, than I could have believed. Drawn from school report cards and job evaluation forms, the 10 MegaSkills make up what

I call "The Never-Ending Report Card."

| | |
|---|---|
| **Confidence:** | feeling able to do it |
| **Motivation:** | wanting to do it |
| **Effort:** | being willing to work hard |
| **Responsibility:** | doing what's right |
| **Initiative:** | moving into action |
| **Perseverance:** | completing what you start |
| **Caring:** | showing concern for others |
| **Teamwork:** | working with others |
| **Common Sense:** | using good judgment |
| **Problem Solving:** | putting what you know into action |

These MegaSkills are our inner engines of learning. They determine our academic and personal success in school and well beyond.

I first wrote about MegaSkills in 1988, *MegaSkills: How Families Can Help Children Succeed in School and Beyond*. This was followed in 1992 with *MegaSkills: The Best Gift You Can Give Your Child*, with a new edition in 1997. These books, which focus on practical activities every family can use to help children achieve, have generated enthusiastic response and led me to the new and complementary MegaSkills teaching strategy in this book that I call MegaSkills Conversations.

Based on the early and strong response to the MegaSkills, I have moved forward to create an innovative and comprehensive training program for educators and parents to help children learn these important basics. Today, years later, MegaSkills is an award-winning, national education initiative sponsored by the Home and School Institute, reaching hundreds of communities. The MegaSkills Conversations of *What Do We Say? What Do We Do?* will have a significant place in the trainings.

MegaSkills program results include higher student test scores, fewer student discipline problems, higher attendance rates, increased time spent on homework, decreased time spent watching TV, and above all, increased participation by all families in their children's education.

It was in listening to families and teachers using MegaSkills activities with children that I came to understand the need for this book. I heard questions.

*Tell us more about what to say, what to do. Give us real situations. Tell us more about how other parents handle problems that come home from school. Tell us what happens when kids come home and cry, "The class is boring."*

*"The teacher doesn't like me." "The other kids make fun of me."*

These may not be end-of-the-world problems, but they can feel like it, when we think back to our own childhoods and remember how, at the time, daily school problems seemed like everything. A lot has changed about growing up and school, but then again, maybe not.

So, I asked myself, how can MegaSkills help us cope better with these everyday problems? What kind of help can I provide? The answer is in this book: real problems, real dilemmas, with real choices for real solutions.

## The Way This Book Works

This book is designed to be an easy-to-use interactive reference. Scenes and "stops" and reminders and questions all through the book encourage ideas and responses.

Each chapter centers on a MegaSkill and has a consistent structure (see page 22). Typical problem situations that come from school to home set the scene. In each chapter there are different school-related problems affecting younger children (approximate grades K–3) and older children (approximate grades 4–6). The age and grade identification are guidelines and not hard and fast categories.

While children's problems set the scene, the focus is on how parents and adults caring for children work with and deal with the problems. Each chapter provides situations and activities to choose among, and talk about, with children. For example, in the chapter on the MegaSkill Effort, the scenario for the younger child is the reluctance to do homework; for the older child, it's a complaint about an unfair grade. These are age-old concerns and they continue to require serious responses.

The book's framework uses what children say and do as "prompts." "Why do I have to do it? What can I do about it?" Using the actual words that children say provides a meaningful link to what adults choose to say and do. This book extends and complements the basic MegaSkills editions. Both are vital in the understanding and use of MegaSkills.

**As you read, think about how you would respond to these concerns and questions, how using your own words, you would explain things differently. That's what I mean about this book being interactive.**

Alongside the conversations between parent and child, there are what I call Reminder Messages. They explain why the adults are saying what they are saying. They're designed to focus our thinking about what we are teaching our children . . . they help us use the special moments presented by the problems as true teaching opportunities. *Look for these Reminder Messages and see how they can be helpful to you. Keep asking yourself what Reminder you may need as you talk with your children.*

At intervals throughout this book, you will also find "Stops." They call for leaving the printed page and moving into action directly with children. They do more than remind us about what we say and do as parents. They immediately move us into action about the topic being addressed.

Check the Reading Together sections in each chapter for recommended books and materials that extend understandings of children and adults about the problems raised in the chapter. These have been assembled especially for this book by Maria Salvadore, Coordinator of Children's Services of the District of Columbia Public Library. In conjunction with the American Library Association, she has developed the lists of MegaSkills-related readings for children and adults for all of the MegaSkills books.

Check the Adult Connections in each chapter. These focus on the ongoing conversations needed . . . between home and school, and how parents and teachers can work together to help children achieve.

The problems and situations discussed are real problems that children typically encounter at different times in their school lives. The responses of adults to the children's pleas follow directly on the page. These exchanges, while scripted, provide a framework from which you build your own personalized answers.

Five essential truths support every word in this book:

**1.** Children are eager to learn and their abilities can be built.
**2.** Parents and caregivers are capable of being great teachers.
**3.** Every home—every home—is a learning place.
**4.** Teachers need and want families as partners in children's education.
**5.** It helps to have a sense about what to say and what to do . . . when those inevitable everyday school problems come home.

## THE CONTENTS / "MENU" FOR EACH CHAPTER

An introduction to the MegaSkill and what we need to teach children about it.

### Younger Child's Situation

Examples: Angela needs to be able to get over being "hurt" by others. Steven needs to be able to learn to pay attention.

### Talking and Doing

Follow-up activities with younger children.

### Older Child's Situation

Examples: Kevin needs to learn how to keep from being bored so easily. Donna needs to get over her fear and desire to be "perfect."

### Talking and Doing

Follow-up activities with older children

### The Adult Connection

Meeting adult needs for school-to-home problem solving.
Example: Whose Homework Is It Anyway?
To Reward or Not to Reward?

### Reading Together

Brief, annotated lists of children's books for parents and children to share together (younger and older children).

## All of Our Children Today . . . and Tomorrow

What happens to children in the book may not yet be happening with your children, but it could . . . if not today, then tomorrow.

For example:

Your child may not be moving to a new school and need initiative to handle the move. Yet, your child needs to use initiative, in all kinds of everyday situations and changes, from meeting a new teacher to making a friend, to using a new bus, to trying out a new food.

Your child may never have direct experience in extending friendship to a handicapped child, but your child has to learn how to express caring.

Your child may not have the specific problems of classmates who are not doing their share, but your child has to learn how to work as a member of a team.

The same is true for all of the examples in this book: They spark our thinking. They help us generalize . . . they build bridges to specific situations in our own lives.

It may sound in this book as if every child rushes home from school eager to tell all. The reality, as we know, is usually very different:

*"What did you do in school today, dear?"*
*"Nothing."*

This is not too different from typical exchanges between husbands and wives:

*"What happened at work today, dear?"*
*"Not much."*

What matters is that we have to get started.

Even as children push adults away, they need us. Children who get into trouble, big trouble, are very often the "quiet, nice kids" who never tell anybody anything.

The children's questions in this book are "starters" for conversations. These are the "What if . . ." kinds of discussions that get kids talking: about themselves and about more than themselves.

From the chapter on Confidence, for example, parents and children talk, even before it happens, about how it would feel when your friends decide that they are not your friends or when you've been number one in the class and suddenly you're not number one anymore.

Being left out; left behind; not being part of the group, especially at school, are real issues for kids. So are the first understandings that everything is not always under their control or the control of their parents. All children, even those who seem to be more confident, are struggling to figure out how the world works and their place in it.

Solid learning takes place in the conversational give and take. As parents we have to talk, but we also learn to listen, and it's not easy, especially when we just want to skip all that and tell our kids what to do.

Real progress gets made in stages, not in one leap from a child's sullen answer, "Nothing," to a full conversation between parent and child. And it doesn't happen at set times. It may happen while we're waiting together for the water to boil or while watching TV or driving in the car. It's for these moments that we need to be prepared. The adult responses in this book help us to become comfortable with a variety of responses to daily problems at school our children have to be able to work on.

## How to Use the Reading Together Sections

Check out the Reading Together sections. You will find these at the end of each chapter. Sharing books is a great way to open up discussions about emotionally charged issues. It is also a great way for children to learn about their own behavior and the behavior of others.

Children's book expert Maria Salvadore, who has assembled the Reading Together books and questions, has selected books for younger and older readers with an eye for diversity and quality. She suggests that parents and teachers keep these tips in mind:

- Ask questions! Keep questions open-ended to encourage discussion. There are no right and wrong answers with open-ended questions, just a variety of responses. (Why do you think Bessie Coleman felt so strongly about becoming an aviator? What do you think made her such a strong character?)
- Ask follow-up questions to draw out other ideas, opinions, and feelings. It is fine to challenge a response if it is done in a non-

threatening way. If you offer an opinion, make it clear that it is your feeling. (I disagree with your opinion, I think Bessie Coleman . . . )

- Discuss the character's action, personality, or problem.
- Even though a book may be heavily illustrated and appear to be more appropriate for younger children, many books work on many levels. Try sharing "younger" books with older children. Discussion questions can be varied and include more worldly questions for older children.

Share books that you like! Remember that as we share books with our children, we reinforce the importance and the pleasure of reading.

## Coaxing Our Children to Talk with Us

How do we coax our children to talk when they don't want to . . . or feel they can't. We can see our youngsters looking all sealed up, closed in, unable to reach out. In this book, it sounds as if they are just waiting to open and talk freely about what's going on and what's bothering them.

Of course, we know it usually doesn't happen that way. There would be long sheets of white paper in this book if I recorded the conversations actually as they take place. To get to the points we need to make, I have to jump over these long pauses and move forward. And I invite you to take that leap with me.

What's in these pages is what it can sound like when parents and children are talking together. So, we have to ask—what can we do to help make it happen? Here are a few suggestions:

- Try not to jump in with "Speak up! What's bothering you?" or words to that effect. This tends to clam up almost everyone.
- Instead, do something together . . . take a walk, go for a swim or a bike ride. Talk about something else altogether.
- Start the conversation in a nonthreatening way. This is like greasing the wheels to get the bike moving smoothly.
- Reveal something about yourself . . . something your child may not have known. Try not to be too obvious—but ask—Has something like that ever happened to you?

Use the problems in this book as discussion sparkers. Invite children to review the story of Paul or Angela or Kim or Steve and ask what they think—the kinds of concerns they have and what kind of advice they would give these kids.

**Children, like adults, find it easier to talk about others before talking about themselves.**

   • Wait, try again . . . keep the conversation going . . . even if it is not yet directly on the troubling issue. The idea is to build trust and confidence it takes to start the process of working through a problem.

Children very early begin to reveal attitudes and behaviors that we know are harmful to their chances for doing well in school and in life. Those little ones, who once wanted to learn about absolutely everything, begin to say:

*"It's boring."*
*"That's not what the TV says."*
*"I hate my school."*
*"My teacher doesn't like me."*

And as youngsters move up in the grades, the words begin to sound like this:

*"I hate to study."*
*"I hate homework."*
*"The other kids aren't doing it."*
*"I've just got to have THAT brand."*
*"I want to go to the shopping center. That's all I want to do."*

It's not too many years later that the words sound like this:

*"As soon as I can drive, I am going to get my own car."*
*"If I want to watch TV all day, nobody can stop me."*
*"When I don't want to go to school, I don't go."*
*"When I don't want to do homework, I just don't do it."*

Advertisers are putting their messages across:

*"Kids, you've just got to have this!"*
*"It's the latest, it's the best."*

And soon these children, many of whom are earning their own money, working at jobs after school, say to their parents and to their teachers:

*"I can do whatever I want to do. This is my telephone."*
*"This is my TV."*
*"You can't tell me what to do. It's my money and I can spend it any way I want."*

This is an escalation process. It doesn't start with arguments about driving a car or having one's own money. It starts when children are much younger and it is dangerous . . . dangerous because children begin to lose perspective and a sense of balance . . . the strength they need for the future.

Can we talk sense to our children? We have no choice. We have to and we can!

The hardest part may not be reaching the children. Children instinctively recognize that the connection to their families is vital; it's a cord that both binds and frees at the same time.

Education has never been more important. For our children to have good jobs in the future and to lead good lives, they need, as never before, to gain a solid education, to become self-disciplined, and to know how to problem solve. Basically, they have to know how to learn and to keep on learning. So do we . . . the adults in their lives.

If we ever wanted a challenge, a climb up Mount Everest, this is IT. It's breathtaking, scary, and exhilarating . . . it's education for children and for parents, together.

**The best is within everyone's reach. It's corny, and it's true.**

# Confidence

# Having It, Losing It, Rebuilding It

## The Mystery of Confidence

**W**HAT IS THIS THING . . . called *confidence.* Some folks have asked that about love. Confidence is also pretty mysterious.

We may be born with confidence, but we sure do a lot of losing it. Then we rebuild it again. It's like an ongoing construction project.

And it's also like a wave . . . it ebbs and flows. A good thing happens and we feel more confident. We fix something or learn something and we feel more confident. Then, a not so good thing happens and we lose that confident feeling.

**Why should we care? Because it matters . . . a lot! Confidence is that all-important belief in ourselves. It enables us to work to be our best and to help others be their best. It enables us to take risks to learn, to achieve . . . to make good things happen and to bounce back when not such good things happen.**

Real confidence rests on a strong foundation. It can't just be a few words of self-esteem that crumple in the first high wind. Real confidence is built incrementally, experience by experience. And that's what every parent can help children learn to do for themselves.

We can't be confident for our children. Worse luck! They have to be confident themselves. We can help put them on the steps of the ladder, but they have to climb it. They have to be the ones to dive off the high board. They have to take the test, give the speech.

Children need to know how to create their own confidence and rebuild it when it needs repairing. They need to know how to keep going. They learn this through observation, through conversation, through direct experience. They learn this from those closest to them.

Do we have to be models of self-confidence to be able to help our children develop confidence? No, thank goodness. But, we do have to be willing to talk about our own sense of confidence, how we get it, how we lose it, how we rebuild it. We have to be able to talk to our children and to encourage them. That's what teaching confidence and all of the MegaSkills are about.

While we can't keep our children from getting hurt or disappointed (much as we would like to), we can help build their resiliency . . . so that when they get hurt, they have the strength to deal with it.

In this chapter, we meet Angela and Paul. They experience typical kinds of disappointments. They happen to almost everyone but they still hurt.

Angela can't understand why her old friends are suddenly turning against her. Paul, who was for a long time number one in his class in sports, no longer finds himself number one.

When children hurt like this, parents hurt, too. When a child comes home from school feeling rejected about what a friend said, or a grade that was not good, or a class office that was lost, it's a hurt that parents feel. Even when we pretend we don't.

What can we do? Can we kiss the hurt away? Sure, and that's good, but we also can do more.

As adults, we can provide the coaching and the cheerleading it takes to help children learn to build and rebuild confidence.

Like good teachers, our job is to help children talk about their experience, to listen, to ask some questions. Very importantly, we are helping children structure their initial emotional reactions into positive, action-oriented responses.

We are helping children be able to say to themselves or to say aloud: "OK: This has happened. It's not great, but I can handle it. What do I do next?"

In our own lives, we can try to set examples. We don't have to be perfect. We may not ourselves jump from the high-dive board, but we muster the courage almost everyday to tackle lots of the things that demand confidence. We apply for a job, we talk to a teacher, we give a presentation. We struggle to turn our own feelings of *I can't* into *I can*. And we need to share these experiences with our children.

Through the questions, answers, and activities in this chapter . . .

- You are building children's understanding about confidence: what it is and how it is built and rebuilt.
- You are helping children learn about other children who have similar kinds of experiences, so that your children know that they are not alone.
- You are sharing your own confidence memories, and how you survived rejection and other not-such-good-things. And look, here you are!
- You are conveying the idea that people are resilient, that not everything has to be perfect in order for it to be good, that tomorrow is indeed another day.

# *When Friends Aren't Friends Anymore*

## (Younger Children)

## *The Story of Angela*

Angela has played with two friends everyday since they were in kindergarten together. They were always in the same classes. They played together at recess. They have been inseparable.

Today, however, something happened. Angela watched as her two friends went off at recess without her. From the other side of the playground, she could see them laughing. Angela was sure that they were talking about her.

She felt terrible. She must have done something awful, but she didn't know what it was, and she didn't know what to do. She started crying. Her teacher saw her and asked, "What's the matter?" But Angela was too upset to talk. Because she had never experienced this before, Angela didn't really know what was the matter. She could feel her whole self sinking. She wished she could evaporate right out of the playground. She wished she could go right home then and there.

Finally, the bell rang and Angela pulled on her sweater and turned as she usually did to walk out with her friends, but they had already left. Angela hated her friends, she hated herself. Angela felt so bad she thought she was going to cry right there at school. It was hard, but she held herself together the rest of the afternoon. But, the minute she walked into her house, she burst into tears.

That night, with her eyes still red and swollen from crying, she told her parents the story of the awful day. Her parents felt terrible. Their daughter's self-confidence had been badly shaken. What could they say? What could they do?

Schools aren't the only place where children have this awful experience of being left out, being excluded. But, for many children, it is the first place where it happens and it has enormous impact on children's attitudes towards school.

On the following pages Angela and her parents talk together about what happened. Angela's parents have this sense that this is really an important learning moment for their daughter . . . and for themselves, too.

**Check the Reminders as you go along. They help in similar kinds of conversations you have with your children.**

## Why Won't They Be My Friends?

*You say that you did nothing to make them angry, and we believe you. But, they may think that you did do something. It could help to find out what that is. Maybe it's all a misunderstanding.*

*Try to remember if anything special happened the last few times you girls were together. Maybe that will give you a clue. If you feel up to it, you could ask them what happened. But, they might not tell.*

*It can be very difficult to be in a trio. There is always the chance that somehow two people in the group will go off by themselves and find something wrong with the third person.*

*Think whether there is a way for you to learn more about what happened. Maybe nothing happened and the girls somehow are just acting mean. But maybe they think there is some reason to be mad at you. It would help to find out what really has happened.*

> **Reminder:** *It can be tempting to urge our children to forget about these kids and find some new friends. That may be bottom line good advice, but it's important to encourage children to try some problem solving first.* ■

## Is It My Fault?

*We wish we could get other people to do what we want them to do—but very often it just doesn't work that way. It's natural to feel unhappy when something like this happens. You don't know why it happened. Maybe you never will really know.*

*But you do know about yourself. You know that you do lots of things right. You have to keep remembering that. Think of all the things you do and you do so well. We'll help you think of them, too.*

*There are times in all our lives when we have to work to keep our spirits up. This is one of these times for you. You are going to do just fine, and we're with you all the way.*

## Can't You Make It All Right Again?

*I wish I could but I can't. I could call up the girls' parents and try to get things patched up. Chances are, it wouldn't last. It would be adults interfering in children's relationships. It usually does not work.*

*You have to do this yourself. You can decide to talk to your friends and try to patch things up. You can decide to forget about them, at least for a while, and make new friends.*

*It's up to you. I can't do it for you. And I know that you can do it. If you want me to, I can tell your teacher what's happened so she can understand when she sees you with other children.*

> **Reminder:** *Oh, how we wish we could smooth our children's way and put a protective seal around them to keep them from getting hurt. It doesn't work, not just because it doesn't save relationships. It doesn't work because our children need the experience of moving forward through difficult situations.* ■

## I Won't Go Back to That Classroom

*It is your class and it's where you have to go. It's just as much yours as it is anyone else's, including the other girls. You will have to be brave.*

*It helps to think about all the things you do right and all the people who like you. Think about the friends you have had and how much you have liked each other. Think about what you can do and are learning to do. Think about your craft projects and your swimming and your bicycle.*

> **Stop:** *Take a few minutes to make up some pep-talk language of your own. One mom who manages a seafood market near a beach tells what happens to her when the market gets too busy. She thinks that she can't handle another order. She just wants to leave the store. But then, she says to herself, "Sure I can. I can do it. Yes, I can do it."*
>
> *Think of a time when you needed a pep talk. Talk about the words of encouragement you can give yourself.* ■

## Maybe No One Will Want to Be My Friend Again

*It's hard for you to imagine this right now because you feel so hurt. But, in a short time, maybe even a few days, maybe a few weeks, you will have new friends. Even though you may not think so now, it just might be that these girls will come back and want to be friends with you again.*

*You know that there are lots of other girls and boys in the class. You have been so busy with the two girls that there's been no time left over for anyone else.*

*You may want to invite some children to come over after school or to go with you to the library or to a movie? You may even want to have a little party. It doesn't have to be fancy and I can help. If you want, we can plan it together.*

*As long as you show that you want to be friendly and that you care about others, have confidence. It may take a little time, but you will have friends.*

> **Reminder:** *Encourage children to think about friendship and what they look for in friends. Children can learn to do the "picking" and not have to wait for others to pick them as friends. It helps to talk about what they are looking for: children who like them, who can be counted on, who are interesting. This early experience in selecting friends is like preventive medicine for the oncoming early adolescent peer-pressure period.* ■

## Did Something Like This Ever Happen to You?

*It certainly did. Let me tell you about the time . . .*

> **Stop:** *Take a few minutes to share an experience or two. What did you learn about yourself and other people? Try to be upbeat even as you share a "down" time.* ■

## Talking Together: What Is Confidence?

When you ask a child to play whom you don't know well, and you feel shy but you do it anyway . . . that's confidence.

When adults try something new for the first time—it could be a new recipe or trying to change a tire—and we are a little frightened, but we do it anyway . . . that's confidence.

These are achievements and we need to take pride in them. That's how we can give ourselves the credit we deserve—credit we can call on for the days that don't go so well and when we need that extra dose of confidence. (See Confidence Bank below.)

**How Do We Show We Have Confidence?**    When we raise our hand in class without being absolutely sure that we have the right answer . . . but we do it anyway; when we play baseball and we're up at home plate to take a swing at the ball, and when we call somebody we don't know and we're scared, but we do it anyway; that's confidence.

When we try . . . even when we don't know in advance if we will succeed; because it just might work, but it won't work at all if we don't try: That's when confidence shows up.

**Confidence Bank:** Together, make a little (or a long) list of confidence achievements with your child. It doesn't have to be "big" to be important. Think of the new things we do, even as little kids: moving from a crib to a bed, moving from training wheels to the two-wheel bike, trying roller-skating and ice-skating and going to camp for the first time and going off to school.

> **Reminder:** *Confidence shows up in such a rich variety of ways as we grow up and older: from a younger child joining a team, to learning to delay immediate gratification; to an older child's being able to stand up to teasing and ridicule and, yes, to question authority, even the authority of home and school. These acts of growing confidence, tempered with growing common sense, are signs of children's evolving maturity. Helping children recognize these achievements as a mark of their own progress is an important parent-coaching role.* ∎

## Doing Together: Talking and Walking Confidence

Our confidence is always being tested. It starts early in the classroom and on the playground.

It's well known how cruel children can be to one another. They haven't learned the art of being subtly cruel without seeming to be cruel . . . so it's straight out teasing and exclusion from groups: "You can't play with us." "We don't like you," and so on.

Children need to be able to defend themselves, even when they are very young. As parents, we help to build these abilities. One of the easiest ways to help children protect themselves from cruelty is to project an air of confidence. It's usually the kids who look weak who are picked on the most. It's unfair, but it's reality.

Confidence shows up in what we say and even how we look. Here's a little game—not really a game but a special way to help children learn how to project confidence in themselves: We can avoid sending the "I am a loser" message to the world just by sending the "I am a winner" message. It takes some practice but all of us can learn to do it. This little game may seem to be too easy to be helpful. But it works.

**Talking:**   First, we say something to each other that shows lack of confidence. It might be "No one likes me." Then, we turn that around into something positive such as, "Mary Jean likes me." Another example can come directly from the playground: "You can't play with us." Then this can be turned into, "That's OK. I'll play with someone else." And so on . . .

**Walking:**   Our bodies show our confidence or lack of it. What does it look like when we are not feeling confident? Is it a slouch? Try it. Now, we turn that into a confident walk. Our heads are up, and we're striding along. Take turns together looking confident.

> **Stop:** *What happened? Did you both try the game? How do you feel? By talking and walking with confidence, do we give ourselves more confidence? What do you think?* ∎

# No Longer Number One

## (Older Children)

### The Story of Paul

Paul has always been a natural when it comes to sports. He just seems to know how to throw and catch a ball. He is usually the first one picked to be on the team. He has always been thought of by others, and by himself, as the best athlete in his class.

This week, a new boy entered the class. Today in gym, he showed that he could run faster than anyone else in the group, including Paul. And he was a better fielder.

The other kids saw that, too, and when it was time for choosing up players for the team, the new boy was the first to be chosen. Paul was among the top picks, but he was not first anymore.

This came as a big blow to Paul. He knew a little about confidence. Everyone had always said that he was so confident. But, today, he didn't feel confident at all. He just felt bad.

That night, it was clear that Paul was upset. He was grumpy. He picked at his food. He was not himself. His parents asked what was wrong. Paul almost didn't want to tell. He felt that bad. But finally they coaxed it out of him, and they sat and talked together.

## It Really Hurts

*Yes, it does, and we thank you for telling us about this and for being brave enough to talk about how you feel. We are not going to tell you not to feel bad. We can't. But, we hope you try not to let this get you way down.*

> **Reminder:** *We need to let our kids know that we value their sharing with us their deep feelings and concerns. It does take bravery to open up and our children need to hear us say so. Even as much as we want to, we can't tell our kids not to feel bad. Feeling bad is part of life. Learning to get over it is a part of life, too.* ■

*You have to keep saying to yourself: "I am going to keep on doing the best I can. Even if I don't do as well as I hope, I won't blame myself."*

*You see ice-skaters on TV. When they fall down, they get right up. It hurts them too—in their legs and in their brains and hearts as well. Even when it's hard, especially when it's hard, we have to keep going. That's the only way we can ever hope to win.*

*What we have to remember is to keep trying and to do our best. When we do, we can't ask for more, and we don't ask for more. You are number one with us, all the time!*

> **Reminder:** *Children can never get enough of hearing that they are number one . . . no matter what. Adults seem to enjoy it, too.* ■

## I Wish the New Boy Never Came

*You can wish it, but it's beyond what you can control. He did better than you did today. Maybe he will always do better and maybe he won't. It would be tempting for us to say to you, "Go out there. You show him. You beat him."*

*Instead, you can try to see the new boy not so much as a competitor but as someone you can learn from. Does he have a special swing that works for him? Think about what he knows and also about what you know. He's new in school and you know the school. You both have lots to teach each other. Try to be friendly with him and see what happens. There is nothing to lose and perhaps a lot to gain.*

## What Are the Other Kids Going to Think?

*You have to try not to worry very much about that. Sometimes we think everybody is looking at us too. But that's called being overly self-conscious— being too concerned about what others are thinking of us. Actually, people are not looking at us all the time or thinking about us. They are busy thinking about themselves.*

*Just as everybody is different, every day is different. Today, you did not come up number one. Tomorrow, you might. But, only if you continue to have confidence in yourself and try not to worry about what others think.*

## Is This Like Not Getting the Absolutely Best Grades?

*Yes, even students who get top grades can't expect to and don't get all As all the time. Some children go home in tears with a report card that includes one B. Some parents look at a really good report card and don't notice all the good marks. Sometimes parents make the situation worse . . . such as, "Why this low mark, why this B?" It's funny when you think about it. All As so rarely happen that it can't be held up as a realistic standard—for anybody, including parents.*

*Different people have different abilities and these can change, too. Let me tell you about what I was good at and not so good at and how it's changed today.*

**Stop:** *Talk together about different strengths at different times. Share from your own experience the balance you have been working to develop—acceptance of your strengths and the areas you need to work on.* ∎

# What Am I Good At?

*A lot of things, and there will be more as you go along. Recognize what you have, and don't worry about what other people have. You have special qualities that others don't have.*

*Think about what you are good at: Remember that you don't have to be great to be good. Give yourself credit for what you can do.*

*What we all need are many ways to achieve. When we become interested and accomplished in a number of areas, including school subjects, and extracurriculars, we are not dependent on just one. It's called broading your interests, and this helps us to feel more accomplished. When we feel we are accomplishing we build multiple confidences. There are many ways of winning.*

> **Reminder:** *While we want our children to be good at something, they don't have to be great at it. They do, however, have to feel good about it and be interested in it, whether it's computers or skating or history. You don't have to be a great gymnast to get pleasure from gymnastics or a great soccer player to enjoy the game.*
>
> *An important educational goal for parents is to help children find something they can become interested in and work at getting better at. In this way, the sentence, "I am learning tennis" is more hopeful in the long run for children's education than "I am a great tennis player." The big issue for educational achievement today and tomorrow is not what you already know, but what you are learning and are capable of learning.* ■

## Why Can't I Be Perfect?

*Well, you can try, but it's highly unlikely that you or anybody or anything can be perfect for long. We don't have to be perfect or number one to do well and be happy.*

*I always tell you to do your best. That's perfect to me, but it's not other people's perfect. It's your perfect when you do the very best you can do at the time. If a test is coming up, and you haven't studied, you are not doing your best. Maybe you will be lucky and get a good grade, maybe not. If you have studied and worked hard to do the best you can do, your grade, even if it is not 100%, rates 100% with me.*

*Sometimes students get so worried about not being perfect that they become afraid to try. There are kids in school, you probably know some, who are afraid to say that they have studied for a test. Instead, they pretend that they didn't open a book. This way, if they get a good grade, they can say, "And I didn't even have to study." They worry that people will think they studied and still didn't do well.*

*A good rule I'd like you to remember is this: Failure is no crime. Not trying is. Win or lose, the main point is how much you try. When you try and even if you fail, you are a winner and we are proud of you.*

> **Reminder:** *Competition has its pluses and minuses. It's useful when it inspires us to do our best. When it becomes jealous rivalry, it doesn't do anybody any good. We need to remind our children (and occasionally ourselves) that the best person to compete against is ourselves, working to become the best we can be.* ■

## Talking Together: Confidence "Secrets"

It's not just children who get scared. Adults have fears to work on and overcome. We don't have to tackle life-and-death issues to have meaningful conversations about fears. One of the strongest ways to build confidence is to start with easier-to-tackle fearful situations. For children, many fearful situations take place in classrooms.

What are children generally afraid of in school? It might be of speaking up in class, asking to be on a team, or trying to get into a group or clique of kids.

What are adults generally afraid of on the job?: Giving a speech, asking for a raise, or learning a new task.

**Share some of these together and talk about these kinds of questions. Feel free to make up more of your own.**

Are people more confident in some situations than others? What is each of us confident about? Do you know what you are good at? Is it math? Is it skating or swimming? What are the reasons for this confidence? Did you take some lessons or did it just come naturally to you?

What do people do that shows confidence and courage? How can you tell? What kind of confidence do you see when you watch TV and see sports stars in action? What kind of confidence do you see on talk shows when participants discuss current events? What do they need to know and how do you think they learn it?

In your own neighborhood and at school, do you see confidence in action? How does it show up . . . in teachers, in students, and in parents?

## Doing Together: The Wonders of Praise

Praise is one of the true miracle workers for all of us, and it's free. The only danger is that we may give it out so freely and generally, especially to children, that it loses its impact. The important point in using praise is to be as specific as possible and to mean what we say!

Here is an easy exercise in using praise—from parent to child, from child to parent, and from child to child (sibling praise rather than sibling rivalry).

Use the following five praising expressions with each other, and be sure to remember to fill in some specifics for each. Trade off with each other, so that you begin an exchange similar to a tennis or volleyball volley. If you laugh while doing this activity, it's OK. The point is to get into the habit of giving praise.

**You did that very well.**
(Pick a specific activity.)

**I'm very proud of you.**
(For what?)

**I knew you could do it.**
(What?)

**You're doing a good job.**
(At what?)

**You're very good at that.**
(What is it and how good?)

Lack of sincerity tends to be recognized. That's why specifics are so important. Make up your own expressions to substitute and/or add to these. Just remember to keep the real praise coming!

# The Adult Connection

## Confidence

## *Confidence About Our Children's School*

It's not just children who need confidence when it comes to school.

Even many of us highly involved parents have admitted, and it's no shame, that we suffer from the old pangs of school anxiety.

Sometimes we don't even know we suffer from this affliction. Memories come back: We think of teachers we didn't like and who didn't like us. We think of the grades that may not have been the greatest; classmates who made fun of us. Our own school memories can be mighty tough on our feelings of confidence, and on our children's schooling, many years later.

These days, this personal anxiety is compounded with general anxieties about how good our schools and our teachers are and whether our children are learning enough. Yet, to be effectively involved with our children's schooling, we have to be able to surmount or suppress a lot of these personal and general anxieties.

Parental involvement has been identified as a major element in children's school success. Readers of this book are already involved or ready to be involved. And we need to give ourselves lots of credit because it takes work, constancy and, yes, restraint and confidence building.

We need confidence not just for ourselves and our children . . . but to improve our schools. To change and reform education, we need to find ways to build the confidence that schools need in order to do the best possible job.

There is today an opposite direction . . . a widespread tendency to worry about and complain about schools. And it's often done loudly in front of the children the school is trying to educate.

Yes, there is much to improve and change in our educational system. Yet, a lot of change has already taken place, usually quietly. What is happening today is often remarkable, effective, and better than it has ever been. This is not often reported in the media because it doesn't make headlines. What makes the news is the discouraging news and it sweeps over all of us and discourages us and diminishes the good work that is being done.

## Both the Advocate and the Critic

The work of an involved parent today includes being both an advocate and a critic, rolled up in one. It's a complex assignment. On the one hand, we need to provide encouragement and confidence building for educators. On the other hand, we need to be their critics . . . critics in the best sense of the word, recognizing what is being done well and identifying what needs to be improved.

There are at least four parts to this complex assignment:

- Recognize what is effective and tell teachers and administrators that we see it and know it and appreciate it. Teachers need a good word, now and then . . . more now than then.
- Share information about what's working at the school, what's new and what's planned, with other parents and with your own children. Become knowledgeable enough to make presentations and advocate for the school at the local school board and state level.
- Become an informed school parent, and if the school does not provide the kind of information needed, ask for it. Schools have not been accustomed to a working partnership role with parents. It's a new job for schools and some of them need reminders.
- Be the critic your school needs: Work with educators to identify the areas for change and help to make these changes happen. Ask for and think about ways you can help, and begin and continue. This takes constancy of purpose, it takes time, and it takes teamwork.

Today, the school-involved parent has moved well beyond the bake sale. We are "growing" a greater number of questioning, concerned parents. This is all to the good, both for the schools, for our children, and for ourselves. It's confidence building in education . . . in a very important, much needed, wider-community way.

# Reading Together:
## Confidence

### Books for Younger Children

*Yo? Yes* by Chris Raschka. Orchard, 1993.
Strong, economical lines and minimal text relate the story of how two boys meet and become friends.

  ● How would you describe each character? Describe each boy's feelings when they meet someone new.

*Will I Have a Friend?* by Miriam Cohen. Illustrated by Lillian Hoban. Macmillan, 1967.
Jim fears that he won't have any friends on his first day of school.

  ● Why is school sometimes scary? How does Jim feel on his first day?

*Heart of a Tiger* by Marsha D. Arnold. Illustrated by Jamichael Henterly. Dial, 1995.
As the Naming Day celebration approaches, a gray kitten strives to achieve a noble name by following the beautiful Bengal tiger through the Indian jungle.

  ● Why are names so important in this story? Why was the tiger reluctant to listen to the small gray cat?

## Books for Older Children

*More Than Anything Else* by Marie Bradby. Illustrated by Chris Soentpiet. Orchard, 1995.

In this fictionalized biography, nine-year-old Booker T. Washington works with his father and brother in the saltworks while dreaming of the time that he will learn to read.

- What obstacles did Booker face? How would you characterize Booker and his family? How would you predict this boy's future?

*Grandfather's Journey* by Allen Say. Houghton Mifflin, 1993.

A Japanese American man and later his grandson have parallel experiences as they journey to a new country.

- Why was confidence so important to these characters? Describe the similarities and differences between grandfather and grandson. Why did they feel torn between two countries?

*Wilma Unlimited* by Kathleen Krull. Illustrated by David Diaz. Harcourt Brace, 1996.

A short, handsomely illustrated biography of the African American woman who overcame polio to become the first woman to win three gold medals in track in a single Olympics.

- Describe how Wilma's family life helped her develop confidence. What other challenges (beyond the physical disability) did Wilma confront?

# Motivation

# The Plague of Boredom

## I Want to Do It!

**I**F CONFIDENCE IS AN internal voice that says, "I can do it," motivation is the voice that says, "I *want* to do it."

We recognize those around us who hear this voice: They have purpose, they are organized, they are involved, they find things interesting, they are enthusiastic, they have goals.

We recognize motivation even as it changes through the years. It's the student who does science experiments even though they are not assigned. It's the employee who offers to help without being asked.

When you take two people with the same basic abilities and opportunities and one keeps moving forward and the other just doesn't seem to get going—the difference is not in their ability, it's in their motivation.

We are motivated, we are born learners. The baby who reaches out to pull at our hair and who pushes things off the table is reaching out to the world, to find out how things work. If we could bottle this motivation from early childhood, repackage it for our growing-up years and hold on to it, then motivation for our children as they grow would not be a problem.

But, it is a challenge and a problem. The problem is that this early motivation needs to be replenished as the years pass and it needs to be reconfigured for the growing years.

Children enter school with tremendous motivation, so eager for the first day that you can feel the motivation vibrations. Something happens along the way through the grades. The first day's eagerness often gets replaced with a malaise and a gripe: "Oh, school is boring," "I don't want to go . . ."

By and large, this is a common problem. It happens not just because school might be regimented or dull. It happens because as children grow older, they have this temptation to say what their friends say: "Everybody hates school."

For children's outside-of-school interests, motivation is usually remarkably strong. This tells us that it is not the motivation that has dried up.

It's really not a mystery about what keeps us motivated . . . especially when we think about what motivates us personally. There are certain basic ingredients:

A sense of *choice,* of self-determination: "I picked that, that's what I want to work on, those are my interests."

The right kind of *challenge,* not too easy and not too hard. Too easy can turn into boredom; too hard can result in anxiety.

*Feedback* that is realistic and focused on specifics. Not the general, "You're a wonderful child." Instead: "You are wonderful at doing such and such."

*Tolerance* for frustration: Who said that our children should never be bored?

In this age of fast-paced entertainment, where movies advertise that the action never stops, it can be hard for children even to tolerate the times in their own real life when the action does stop. It can get very easy for a child to say, "I'm bored," and for parents to somehow feel a twinge of guilt and frustration about it.

Forget this guilt. We cannot be motivated for our children and we can't keep them from feeling bored . . . if that is what they want to feel. The best we can do, and it's a lot, is to help children take charge of their own motivation and to see their own responsibility for being interested and motivated.

Laura is an only child. Now that she has started school, she is in a group for the first time, and it shows. She acts bored and distracted. Her teacher is concerned and has asked her parents for help.

Kevin finds just about everything in school "boring," and he's made no effort to conceal his feelings. His teacher is very worried about him. He's disorganized and he's discouraged. At the parent-teacher conference, his teacher asked his parents to have a serious conversation with him. In this chapter, the focus is on fostering motivational strength within children so that they have greater internal capacity to deal with inevitable discouragements, to keep on going, and to feel beauty and excitement on even the most "boring" days.

Through the activities and conversations in this chapter:

* **You are building your children's ability to fight boredom, by mobilizing their own enthusiasm and motivation for learning.**

* **You are helping children build their own storehouse of encouragement that will make them able to dispel discouragement and disappointment.**

* **You are helping children understand their own responsibility for keeping interested and for taking charge of their own attitudes.**

# A Lot of Everything

## (Younger Children)

### The Story of Laura

Laura has always had a lot of everything. As an only child, she is the apple of her parents' eye. They waited a long time to have her. Laura's parents are very generous—with their gifts and attention, and Laura goes everywhere with them.

In a picture taken of Laura on her first birthday, she is sitting in the midst of a mountain of presents. She looks as if she is lost. Her face has a confused look; it's as if she doesn't know which way to turn, which one of the mountain of presents she should open and play with first. It was that way again on her second birthday, and then her third, and fourth birthdays: always surrounded by another mountain of gifts, always looking just the tiniest bit dazed.

Last year on Laura's first day of kindergarten, her parents gave her special gifts to mark the day; and they went with her to school. She liked kindergarten but always seemed to feel that she was not being "liked enough." This year, on her first day in first grade, Laura came home crying. "The teacher didn't pay attention to me."

Laura's parents went to school to meet with the teacher. They expected to hear that Laura was the darling of the class, just as she was the darling at home. What they heard was very different.

The teacher said that Laura demands a great deal of attention; that she flits from one corner of the room to another, that she can't seem to focus, that about a minute into any activity, she whines that she is bored.

Her parents decided to tell Laura what the teacher said. Laura kept on interrupting and running away into the other room. For the first time, her parents saw what her teacher saw. While Laura wanted all the attention, she was herself not paying attention. The following pages reveal what her parents explained to Laura over several conversations.

## The Teacher Doesn't Pay Attention to Me

*You're used to getting a lot of attention . . . maybe even too much. At home, you get all the attention.*

*In the classroom, the teacher has to pay attention to many children, not just to you. So, it may feel that she is not paying attention. But she really is.*

*We know because she was able to tell us a lot about you and what is happening with you and for you in class.*

*Just because the teacher isn't always noticing you all the time or calling on you a lot doesn't mean that she isn't paying attention to you. You can't expect to get the same kind of attention at school that you get at home. At home, we can pay attention and talk to each other a lot because there are only the three of us. In school, your teacher has to pay attention to and try to talk to all the children in the class. She is noticing you even when she isn't talking to you or calling on you.*

## What Did the Teacher Say About Me?

*Well, she said that you have trouble concentrating, that you run around in the class, that you don't finish your assignments.*

*She said that you seem bored. And that worries her.*

*She says that sometimes children say they are bored when they cannot do the work. But, she believes that you are capable, and she urged us to tell you that she thinks so and wants you to show how capable you are.*

## The Teacher Told Me That I Need Motivation. What Does That Mean?

*It means that the teacher thinks you have other things on your mind and that you are not paying enough attention at school. It means that the teacher thinks you don't want to do enough at school.*

*Your teacher cares about you and wants you to do well. So do we. We know that you want to learn, and that once you get used to school, it will come easier for you.*

*I want you to try to remember that the motivation the teacher was talking about is inside you. You have the power to pay attention and to find things interesting and to want to learn. We are going to help, but we can't be motivated for you. Maybe that is what we have been trying too hard to do.*

*Everyday I have been asking you to talk about how you are doing at school. It is really more important to ask about what you are doing and what you are becoming interested in. I want to know, and I want you to want to tell me. It really doesn't have to be anything you learned. It might be something funny you want to share.*

**Stop:** *Talk a bit about setting goals for yourself and how that helps you keep on task and stay motivated. Tell about how you use goals and assignments to help you do what has to be done. For example, cooking is a daily activity, but you literally add spice to it by learning new dishes, and this keeps you interested in learning more. It's true for every subject—the more we learn, the more there is to know and to keep on learning. Children can begin to learn this at an early age, little by little.* ■

## I'd Rather Be Home Playing . . .

*You will get a chance to do the things you want to do, but not all of the time. The teacher wants to know about the special things you like to do. But, most of the time, you will do what the whole class does. When it's reading, it's reading time. When it's math, it's math time. That's the way school is. You will get used to it and you will find that you enjoy it.*

*When you are home and you're watching television and you get bored with a show, you change the channels. But, when you are at school, there is no changing channels. You are in the class and that is where you do your work.*

*We will talk together about the things you find more boring and more interesting, and we'll do more of the interesting things. But not everything you do will interest you all the time. When we stick with things, they can get more and more interesting.*

## I Don't Want to Do What the Teacher Says . . .

*When you are in the school and you are part of a class, you do things that the whole class does, not all the time, but a lot of the time.*

*There is work to do that everyone has to do. You have subjects to learn and books to read and projects to do. There is a program that you and your classmates follow.*

*Your teacher expects you to raise questions and to want to do other things as well as the assignments she assigns. That's the point—you have to do your assignments. Then you may be able to do the other things you want to do.*

## Will I Ever Get to Like School?

*We think so, lots of kids do. We know that it's hard to get used to the routine of school, to having to share things with the other kids, to having to listen to and do what the teacher says. We know that it takes getting used to. But, you do have to get used to it. You are now a member of a class. You are not just our little girl. You are part of the school group.*

*You may not always like to do what you are asked to do in school, but the school has rules to follow and you will learn to follow them.*

*When the rules are silly or unfair, we can talk about them and talk with the teacher. But, most of the time, they will be fair and important for the whole group.*

*The good part of being in a larger group is learning and studying together and having fun together and just plain being part of something big.*

> **Reminder:** *Yes, children can get frustrated in school. For example, some children learn to read so quickly and so well that it's almost torture for them to sit still and wait for the other kids to catch up. Other children need more time to read and feel frustrated when they can't keep up with the class.*
>
> *There is no easy answer for these situations. There is a lot of discussion about individualized attention for each student, and it is the ideal that all good teachers strive for. But, it's tremendously difficult to achieve . . . and doesn't happen every day.*
>
> *So, what's to be done. First, this is no time to be shy. Parents and children have to speak up. The child who is always waiting for the others needs more challenging assignments. The child who is lagging much of the time needs more help. The key words here are "always" and "much." (Teachers*

*and parents need to hear about continuing patterns of prob-*
*lems and not about a one-day situation.)*

*Ask to talk with the teacher. If possible, invite your child*
*to join you. This can be a real growing-up experience. Talk*
*about practical steps that can be taken now, one by one, in*
*school and at home.*

*In the meantime, tell children to calm down and remember*
*that having to wait a bit is not a terrible thing and that*
*feeling frustrated for a relatively short time is not a terrible*
*thing either.* ■

## *Talking Together: Learning/Doing Something New*

Was there something we both learned recently?

Did you learn something new? Think hard . . . skating, jogging, cooking, computing

Did I learn something new? Let me think . . . reading, swimming, biking, sewing

Did I talk you into something that at first you didn't want to do? And vice-versa . . .

What makes your friends want to do something? When they want to play a certain game, do you always want to?

How do they get you to do it? How do you talk them into something they might not want to do at first?

When you really want to do something, how do you feel?

## Doing Together: Watching and Wondering

Most of the time we are running so hard and our days are so filled that there is hardly any time left just to sit, just to think, even a little.

Motivation needs replenishment. How we wish there were a motivation vitamin . . . but there is an exercise that can help. It may not seem as if it builds motivation, but it does in a quiet, personal way.

This is a very different activity—it calls for watching quietly. The idea is to look at the sky, a tree, a passing car, a butterfly—whatever takes our fancy. For adults, too, this is a motivation renewal exercise.

Start with a minute or two and build up to five or ten minutes, whatever the schedule will bear.

Go for walks with your child. As you walk along, pay special attention to the different shops you see and the work being done. Supermarket clerks, truck drivers, bakers, florists, waiters, construction workers . . . everything that goes on all around us every day . . . that we are often too rushed to notice. Talk about what you see and the contribution those people are making to the life of your community.

# "It's Boring!"

## (Older Children)

## The Story of Kevin

When Kevin's parents went in for their parent-teacher conference this fall, his teacher said,

> *"Kevin just isn't motivated. He sits there and mutters and sometimes says aloud, 'I'm bored.' Even when he doesn't say it, he looks bored and doesn't participate. He often stares out the window. When he's working on an assignment and he doesn't get it right away, he gives up easily.*
>
> *"It's really worrisome, and it may not just be a passing thing. It's bad for Kevin and frankly it's bad for the whole class. We can't just let this happen.*
>
> *"I'm ready to work with you. I think it's very important that you have some real conversations with Kevin to find out what's going on. Then come back and talk with me. We need a plan to be able to help Kevin. We need to work together."*

This wasn't the first time Kevin's parents heard about his lack of motivation. This judgment about him has been following him from grade to grade, but never had a teacher been so worried before, and never had a teacher put it to his parents that this was serious and that they needed really to talk with their son to find out what was on his mind.

His parents were encouraged by the teacher's willingness to help, but they weren't sure about what they were going to say to their son. They felt anxious, they were worried and disappointed.

After dinner they told Kevin that they had been to his school. They told him about what the teacher said and encouraged him to comment on what he was hearing and to ask questions.

## Why Can't I Say, "I'm Bored"?

*For one thing, it is very easy to say, "I'm bored." It doesn't mean very much and it makes the other people you are with, including the teacher, feel uncomfortable.*

*It's as though you are expecting them to keep you un-bored. And that is too much to expect of other people. The only person who is able to un-bore you is yourself. You have to find interest in the things you are doing, and you can. That is what motivating yourself is about. So, what you have to do is figure out why you are saying that you are bored. For instance, if you are feeling bored about a project you are doing, it might mean that the work is too easy for you. Or, it might mean that the work is hard, and you don't want to work hard to figure it out. When you can tell us and tell your teacher what makes you feel bored, then we can all try to do something about it.*

> **Stop:** *Remind children about when they show motivation. Example: Some kids may find math in school a real trial but love sports so much that they work daily with team scores and batting averages. Others write comic strips, stories, or poems at home but dread writing in class.*
>
> *Children need to know when they show motivation, because it can be that they are not aware of these strengths. From one strength, we go on to build other strengths. Children who are enamored of trucks or cars or airplanes can move with these interests to geography and science and history. There are connections in all of these learnings.* ■

## Why Pick on Me? All the Kids Say They're Bored.

*Well, we know you and we care about you. We're not picking on you. We're trying to help. Our concern is this: When people keep saying over and over that they're bored, they might start to believe it. Then, it gets harder and harder to find things interesting.*

*To get interested in something takes work. Most of us start out not being very interested, until we learn more about something or start to practice it more and more.*

*Getting better at something actually helps us get more motivated. When we first start doing something, anything, from reading to jogging, we're not very good at it. At first, we don't read fast or run fast. But, by doing it more and more, we build up our abilities and our interests.*

*The danger of saying over and over, "I'm bored," is that it may keep us from starting things and from finding out what we are really interested in.*

> **Reminder:** *Interests lead to abilities and then to more interests. Most of us are not immediately artists or great sports stars. We have to work at developing our abilities and as we do it, we become more and more interested. Many lifelong interests get started that way. Many engineers and scientists tell about how they got started with erector and chemistry sets their parents brought home when they were little children.* ■

## Were You Bored in School?

*Sure, I got bored, and I wish I knew when I was a kid what I know now about what we have to do to fight boredom. I don't have all the answers but I know that we have to struggle against feeling bored.*

*We have to try to find things interesting. Even in school, we have responsibilities for making things less boring. For example, you might be sitting in a class that is not too interesting. What can you do? It would not be a good idea to jump up and shout. But you can ask a question or two, and it might get a lively discussion going.*

*I wish all teachers were more concerned about and able to keep classes lively and involving. We can't always count on that. So, we have to count on ourselves to help.*

*We can talk with the teacher about having more participation, more activities to do . . . students can take on some responsibility for making the class more interesting. We need to try to make the most of every class we are in.*

## I Wish I Was Never Bored

*Sure, I wish that, too. But, that's not realistic. When we watch TV or go to the movies, there is something exciting happening every minute.*

*We can get the idea that there is never anything to be bored about. But, we don't see what happens all day long. We usually don't see the hero doing everything all the rest of us do . . . eating, sleeping, reading. In movies and on TV, the everyday stuff is edited out and all we see are the few moments when something interesting is happening.*

*But, it's not the way it is. There needs to be time for quiet, for thinking, for studying. Much of that is not going to be exciting, nor should we expect it to be. The truly exciting times in everyday life are the exceptions, not the rule.*

*And that's probably all to the good. We need busy time and we need quiet time, too.*

> **Reminder:** *Teachers are worried these days that kids expect to be entertained too much in school. At home, parents worry that children think daily life is supposed to be similar to TV. As long as we keep talking, our children will have more realistic views about what to expect.* ■

## What Will Motivate Me?

*Start where you are. What do you like to do? Or wish you could do?*
*Do you admire certain people and want to learn more about them?*
*Do certain kinds of jobs interest you and do you want to learn more about them?*
*Do you like a certain sport and want to learn more about it?*

*Asking yourself these types of questions can help you to set goals. And setting goals is very important in motivating ourselves.*

*While it's good to have a goal, it needs to be realistic and not be overwhelming. If you're thinking about getting all As, for example, and now you're mostly getting Cs, you may need to get some Bs first.*

*It means figuring what steps to take to meet your goal. If you want to be able to run a mile in a certain number of minutes, you need to figure out what kind of progress is needed week-by-week.*

*To keep ourselves motivated, we have to be able to notice and measure our own success along the way. When people go on diets, they weigh themselves regularly in order to be able to know how well they're doing. This builds their motivation to keep going.*

*I'll work with you. We'll be on the lookout for a hobby or two that maybe we can do together. It can be anything from exercise, to sports, to woodwork. It will be something we can both do.*

> **Stop:** *Tell about a special interest or two you had when you were a child. How did it get started? Was there a special person or special event that helped you begin?* ■

## Talking Together: What Did You Do Today?

In this activity, the child gets to ask the parent: *What did you do today?* It's a reverse turn on the often-asked question for children: *What did you learn in school today?*

While we can't just give kids motivation, we can enable them to share our interests and the things that motivate us. We don't have to recount anything big or exciting. In fact, if the day was just ordinary and most days are, that's what we ought to say. Children need to hear from us what is real and not depend on movies or TV to paint the picture of the world for them. It's not all fun and games and action. Days at work and at home can be pretty dull, and that's not terrible. Adults learn to live (and sometimes enjoy) a certain amount of boredom, and so can children.

Try to focus more on the positive rather than on the negative. This means that we look for the special moments of the day and we concentrate on sharing those. It might be the unusual sandwich at lunch or the funny scene we saw on the way to work. It might be the new computer program on the job or the new boss or the old friend who drops by to say "hello." It doesn't have to be a big event to be interesting.

Children will get the idea from this sharing that they can tell about the small events, too, and little by little the enthusiasms of their day will begin to come through.

**Stop:** *Keep a note or two so that you don't forget to tell about a special moment that you want to share with your child.* ■

## Doing Together: The Encouragement List

This activity has children motivating their parents. Usually it's the child who receives motivating words from parents and teachers. But, motivation need not be a one-way street from parent to child.

Here are some words that might make the list good for parents as well as children:

| | |
|---|---|
| Proud | Keep it going |
| Super | You can do it |
| Great | I really appreciate that |
| Excellent | Etc., etc. |
| Marvelous | |

To play the game, at least one praise word needs to be said aloud once a day by parents to children—and by children to their parents. Be as specific as possible so that these are not empty words.

For example, parents can start: "You made me very **proud** today when, without being asked, you helped me carry in the heavy grocery bags from the car."

And then it's the child's turn: "You made me feel **super** when you told me how much you liked the story I wrote for school."

And then the parent's: "**I really appreciate it** when you make sure that the breakfast dishes get put away in the morning."

Then the child's: "I think it's **great** that you remembered to buy me my favorite dessert at the store."

Talk out the encouraging words, write them down. Be sure to post them where they can be seen and enjoyed.

# The Adult Connection

## Motivation

## To Reward or Not to Reward

Do rewards build or destroy motivation? Is giving grades a good idea? How does money and recognition work in all of this? What about incentives? What about privileges?

So much time is spent worrying about what the reward is that we can forget the larger question. It's the question about the *message* sent by the reward.

MegaSkills experience tells us that it really makes little difference what the reward is—whether it is grades or money or praise. The big issue is its message.

Rewards are neither good nor bad things to give, when they provide what our children need—ways to help teach the attitudes and behaviors to provide opportunities for fulfilling lives.

The right kind of rewards at the right time can be helpful. They can help to teach and reinforce hard work, dependability, increased academic competencies, and constructive personal and social behavior.

What we look for is a kind of system, whether we call it a reward system or not. It's a way to reinforce attitudes and behaviors that we believe in and that we want our children to believe in and act on.

Whatever reward system we pick, it has to fit what we are trying to teach. Just as "the punishment is supposed to fit the crime," the reward needs to try to fit the behavior we are seeking to support. And there needs to be a level of consistency, so that children know what to expect.

> **Rewards build motivation when they build children's appetites to develop . . . and when this development is strong enough to continue even though the rewards are withdrawn. Rewards can destroy motivation when they become the only reason that children work hard at home or do well in school. The danger is that when the reward stops, the child's motivation stops. That's when the reward does not fit the behavior we hope to teach.**

Rewards can have a negative impact when they are overdone. I get concerned about reward systems that, for example, pay children every time they read a book. It worries me that the message gets conveyed that we read only when we get paid.

When a child gets a good grade at school, does that automatically mean a trip to the store for a gift? I worry about the message we send when we go on automatic this way. Too many gifts along the way can detract from the big reward of meeting the goal.

Children deserve encouragement and praise, but we need to help children stretch out their ability to keep going. When rewards help children understand that there is a payoff for working hard and achieving better grades, then the reward is doing an important job.

We can learn to reward ourselves and not have to depend on others to reward us. Children can learn this. It works best to have a goal (it might be getting a better grade in school or exercising or learning a new sport). Then we figure out a step-by-step plan (it can be a modest, simple plan) to achieve it. We start the action. We check our progress at regular intervals. Are grades going up? Are muscles becoming stronger?

Some people can keep at something without having to have an external reward to keep going. Most of us need it. And there is no shame in needing rewards.

Ideally, especially for children, we have to try to match the reward to the goal being worked towards. For example, when the goal is better grades in English, the family reward can connect with that goal, in the form of books, videos, family visits to museums and libraries.

There is a reward often used by schools that, I believe, really sends the wrong message. Sometimes schools give out the reward of not having to do homework. This sends a message that is contrary to what we want to put across. It says that homework is a punishment that we have to try to avoid. A better reward, if homework is to be used in this way at all, is to design a homework assignment that uses a pleasurable activity outside school such as a trip to a museum or even to a supermarket. A really good homework assignment that builds on and extends children's real interests is a joy and reward.

And let's not forget that spending time together is a reward, too. Children across the nation, when asked what they want most from their parents, answered in one word: Time!

Outside my window, almost every day, when the weather is good, a group of young boys play street hockey. It's not a regular game. It's practice. They are as motivated as any group I have ever seen. They are not getting grades, but they are getting something stronger: They are getting better and better.

This group is an inspiration to me. The last time I looked the seven-year-old was the goalie, and he managed to block almost every puck. He had started at this position only a month before and the pucks used to whiz past him. Clearly, he has talent, but most of all, he has old-fashioned grit and remarkable determination. He knows what he wants: He is motivated to get there, and he will.

These boys may not, in their golden years, remember this hockey practice exactly, but it will last them all their lives. It will not be their biggest accomplishment in their lives. But it is an important stepping-stone to the inner rewards that will be a continuing resource all through their lives.

May all our children have such experiences. It need not be hockey, but let it be something that builds that wondrous inner motivation inside every child.

# Reading Together:
# Motivation

## Books for Younger Children

*Crow Boy* by Taro Yashima. Viking, 1955.
Throughout his school years, Chibi is shunned by the other children until they learn the difficulties he overcame to achieve perfect attendance.

- Why was school so important to Chibi? How did the teacher support him? Why were the children afraid of Chibi?

*Edward's Overwhelming Overnight* by Rosemary Wells. Dial, 1995.
Edward's parents tell him that because of the snow, he'll have to spend the night at his friend's house.

- Why was Edward so reluctant to spend the night? How do his parents feel about Edward's overnight? Why do Edward's parents know he will be ready some day?

*Lilly's Purple Plastic Purse* by Kevin Henkes. Greenwillow, 1996.
Lilly loves everything about her school, especially her teacher. But when he asks her to wait a while before showing her new purse, she does something for which she is later sorry.

---

- Why doesn't Lilly want to wait to share her excitement? Why does her teacher make her wait? How do the other children in class respond?

## Books for Older Children

*Fanny's Dream* by Carolyn Buehner. Illustrated by Mark Buehner. Dial, 1996.
Fanny Agnes is a sturdy farm girl who dreams of marrying a prince but decides on a local farmer when her fairy godmother doesn't show up.

- How did Fanny make her dream come true? How do dreams grow or change as people grow and change?

*JoJo's Flying Sidekick* by Brian Pinkney. Simon & Schuster, 1995.
Everyone gives JoJo advice on how to achieve her yellow belt in tae kwon do classes, but ultimately, she figures it out for herself.

- What does the "bandit tree" symbolize for JoJo? How does her fear motivate her? How does JoJo's success help prepare her for future challenges?

*Patchwork Quilt* by Valerie Flournoy. Illustrated by Jerry Pinkney. Dial, 1985.
Using scraps from the family's old clothing, Tanya, her grandmother, and her mother make a quilt to tell the family story.

- Why did they decide to make a quilt? Why did Tanya continue on the quilt even after her grandmother became ill?

# Effort

# Homework and Beyond

## The "Look" of Effort

**I**N CLASSROOMS ACROSS THE nation, I ask the same question of children from kindergarten to grade six. I invite them to show me in drawings what effort looks like and what it doesn't look like.

Their drawings go onto pieces of paper that are divided in half vertically. At the top of one column is the word *NO*. On the other side is the word *YES*. For the *no* column, children are told to draw what no effort looks like. In the *yes* column, the children are asked to draw what real effort looks like.

The results continue to amaze me. We don't talk about effort in advance. The kids receive no lectures about it. But, from kindergarten on up, children know what effort is. They can show it.

Despite the fact that children plead to watch TV, they know that TV is a no-brainer and takes no effort. The kids in the drawings on the *no* side are lying down watching TV and munching candies or popcorn. Children are shown alone, not with friends or family members. Moreover, they don't look as if they are having fun.

On the other hand, the drawings on the *yes* side all indicate a high level of activity. The kids in the pictures actually look as if they are having fun. There are pictures of kids throwing footballs surrounded by people in a crowded stadium. There are kids feeding their pets. There are kids taking out the garbage and actually smiling.

This may not be the most scientific of studies, but it suggests certain very positive findings. Children understand the value of effort. They know more than we think they do.

To be sure, getting a child to throw a football or take care of a pet may be considered easy efforts. There is a readily understood pleasure involved. Taking out the garbage and picking up trash is a harder sell. Perhaps the hardest sell of all is the old standby: homework.

## The Sound of Effort

*I can't do it. I won't do it. It's too hard. I don't like it. I hate the teacher. I hate school.*

It's 3 P.M. and the sound of homework has begun to be heard in the land . . . generally it's not a happy sound.

It doesn't take long before parents hear those predictable words: "Won't you help me?" "Why won't you help me?" "If you were a 'good' parent, you would help me." And that in turn brings us to this question: When it comes to homework, what does being a good parent really mean?

As good parents, our goal must be to help our children make more of an effort . . . not just on homework, but it is a start. Above all, we have to help our children understand the satisfaction of effort.

Effort enables us to get something done. It has the added benefit of making us feel good. We feel proud of ourselves, we feel more complete. That's what effort does for us—and that's the message children understand about football and clubs.

It's not as readily understood about homework. Probably because doing homework does not provide the immediate big bang of catching a pass. The achievement in homework comes much later with graduations and in life beyond school. It's no wonder it's harder for young children to see it.

> **Reminder:** *Kids need time, just as adults do, to get their work done. There is a growing pattern of loading kids up on extracurricular activities to give them more to learn and to keep them out of trouble, too. These extra activities can be constructive and interesting, but they do take time.*

*Many children want to sign up for everything. There's Scouts and soccer and ballet and so many clubs it's hard to keep track. For some kids who thrive on being very busy and doing it all, this can be fine. But for others, it can be too much. They need to be able to concentrate and need the time to do well in a few areas.*

*There is no one right answer to fit all kids, but there is one basic question. It's this: Will there be enough time (not just for the parent to take the child to all the activities) for the child to make the serious effort needed to learn both the extracurriculars and the curriculars? If yes, fine. If no, that's fine, too. All the more reason to think about this in advance.* ■

Children benefit most when they understand why it is in their own interests to exert effort. Through these activities and conversations in this chapter:

● You are building a base of understanding about *effort*, what it is, how it works, for adults as well as children.

● You are reinforcing the message that *effort* and hard work are important.

● You are making it clear that there are different kinds of *effort*, from bike riding to schoolwork.

● You are letting your child know that you, even as an adult, may not always want to make that extra effort. But that you do it anyway because *effort* is what has to be done.

● You are reaffirming your belief that your child is capable of *effort* and that you and your children are partners in this work.

# The Homework Hassle

## (Younger Children)

## The Story of Tim

Tim is a likable young fellow, especially when he gets his own way. And he gets it a lot.

He is also the big brother in the family, with a baby sister just learning to walk. Both parents work outside the home and both are involved with Tim's school.

In kindergarten and first grade, Tim did very well; he had favorite subjects and didn't have to work very hard to bring home good reports. He didn't have any homework at all until he entered second grade. When he used to come home from school before he had homework, he would spend almost all of his time outdoors playing with friends and then watching his favorite TV shows before bed.

So, when Tim started getting homework, it really came as quite a jolt. Tim didn't like to have to give up playtime and his TV shows. And he didn't see why he had to do it. In fact, almost every night there would be some kind of scene as Tim, cranky, tired, and impatient, would fidget and fuss and just dash through his assignment.

His parents, shocked by his lack of interest and exhausted by the evening arguments, began to dread the nights when Tim had work to do. It's not that the homework was very long and complicated. In fact, it didn't matter much to Tim at all how hard the assignment was . . . he just didn't want to do it.

## Homework Is Boring. Why Do I Have to Do It?

*To tell you the truth, I didn't always enjoy my homework, either, when I was in school. I made some of the same fuss that you are making.*

*I agree with you that homework can get boring. I am not going to pretend that it can't. But homework does very important things for us—it helps us get into the habit of organizing our things and managing our time. It helps give us the practice we need to make sure we understand what we are doing. It makes sure we have the time it takes to learn.*

*For example, when you know you have homework, you have to think to yourself: How much time will it take? What supplies do I need? You have to make that time and find those supplies and then you have to concentrate. You have to focus on the homework and turn off the TV and not talk on the phone and then get the work done. It doesn't always take a lot of time. I know that it's not always fun, but it is your job.*

> **Reminder:** *Even when children complain that they know the material and the homework is a waste of time, remind them that doing the homework is not a choice, that when they do their homework, they are "proving" to themselves and their teachers that they can indeed make the effort.* ■

## I Don't Like My Teacher

*Sometimes we like people more and less on different days. Some days you tell me that you like the teacher. Some days you don't. It feels good to like your teacher, but you don't have to—and you certainly don't have to all the time.*

*You have to remember that your teacher isn't just* your *teacher. Your teacher is the teacher for the whole class and that means that sometimes others in the class get more attention than you do.*

*But, no matter how you feel on any one day, you have to do the work whether you like the teacher or not.*

**Reminder:** *Teachers have bad days and good days too—just as we all do. If your child and teacher are having difficulties over a long period of time, not just a few days, make an appointment to go in together to see the teacher. It's important that we don't let difficult situations get worse . . . when we can solve problems early on.* ■

## The Baby Gets to Play All Day

*When you were a baby, you played a lot and you still play a lot. But now you have to find time for work. That is part of growing up and it's good. It helps you grow.*

## Do You Have to Do Things You Don't Want to Do?

*Of course. It's not always so easy for adults to make an effort. We don't always do what we want to do. I don't always want to make dinner or go to work. Some days I would rather go to the movies.*

*I do what I have to do, even when I don't want to, because our family needs me. And, because I love you.*

**Stop:** *Share with your child more examples of what you do . . . even when you don't want to. Invite your children to tell you some of the same.* ■

## I Don't Want to Do That Homework Again. It's Good Enough.

*Maybe it is, maybe it isn't. I just want you to know that I often have to do things over because they weren't good enough the first time. I don't believe everything has to be perfect, but it does have to be good. You need to give it your best effort. It has to be your best, not just something you might be tempted to call your best. When you do that, then it's good.*

*Basketball players practice and practice. Musicians practice and practice. They know they have to keep working to do their best.*

*We need to take pride in what we do. We need to be able to say: "That's the best I can do today!" And if it takes more than once or twice to do "the best I can do"—then I need to be willing to do it.*

## Do I Work Hard?

*You often ask us, "Do we work hard?" And I say, "Often you do." You work hard to learn a new game. You work hard on your favorite school subjects. And you've said to us, "That doesn't seem like effort!" But, it is.*

*But, often you come home from school and say: "This is too hard. You have to help me."*

*And then we say, "You can do it. Make an effort." We say this because there is a wonderful feeling all of us get when we work to make something happen, when we accomplish something, when through our own efforts we see something get done. It's a terrific feeling when we can say: "I did that!" And that includes homework.*

## Can Hard Work Ever Be Fun?

*Absolutely. Sometimes what seems like fun is really hard work. It doesn't feel like hard work when you're practicing your swimming or riding your bike. Does it?*

*When we pick jobs to do, we try to pick what we like to do and what we are good at. But, not everything we do is fun.*

*People work hard in different ways. Some people work hard at being teachers. Other people work hard driving a tractor or a truck. Other people work hard as lawyers, doctors, or salespeople. Believe me, parents work hard, too.*

*When you like what you are doing, work can feel like fun. We don't enjoy working all of the time, but we do have to get things done. When what we have to do gets done, we have the time to do other things that we want to do.*

*This takes effort. We need to get into the habit of making this effort. Then, almost like a miracle, it doesn't seem like so much effort.*

> **Reminder:** *We need to let our children know that even when we like what we are doing, there are parts of it that we don't like, even for hobbies. When we paint pictures, we have to put out our paints and clean up afterwards. Our children can come to understand that there is "no free lunch." With pleasure comes effort. When we understand this, we can appreciate the pleasure even more.* ■

## Talking Together: How Do We Know When We Are Working Hard?

Discussion sparkers help keep the conversation going about effort. Here are five questions with key ideas in bolder print. Share your own experiences as you ask your children to share theirs. No idea is out of bounds. This is an opportunity to bounce ideas around, a way to hear ourselves think.

What kind of **efforts** do we make **for ourselves**?
What kind of **efforts** do we make **for others**?
How do we **know** when we are **working hard**?
Who are the **people** we know **who work hard**?
What do we do that is **fun** and **hard work at the same time**?

> **Stop:** *Talk about what you do and what your child does that takes effort and still feels like fun! The list can get mighty long. Read aloud or tell the story of Tim and his problems with homework. Ask for your child's ideas on how to help Tim understand the importance of effort.* ■

## Doing Together: Special Time/Special Place

Every child needs a special place in which to be a student; a place ideally suited for the *effort* of homework. It need not be fancy to do the job.

Study-time need not be long for young students. It's best when it can be regular, at a certain time each day. Consistency and stability are important basics.

- Develop with children a schedule for homework and for chores around the house. List these on a calendar, day-by-day, week-by-week.
- Convey the impression that your children can do the job. If they are hesitant, remind them of previous accomplishments. Be encouraging, and be specific.
- Pick the time for homework with care. In some homes, early morning is the best time; in others, it's after supper. TV should be off and the telephone off limits.
- Help children, as needed, to break down a job into manageable steps. This is true for household jobs like cleaning their room to doing big homework assignments.
- Don't expect perfection. When children ask you to look at their achievement, from skating a figure eight to completing a math assignment, praise but don't overdo. If you have criticisms, make them, but gently.
- Make the point and keep making it: Education is important. Let children know that this is what you value.

# Homework and Heartache

## (Older Children)

### The Story of Jessica

It would be grand if effort were straightforward: We know what needs to get done, we get right down to it, work hard, and complete our task, get praised and rewarded. Yet as we get older, effort—like many other things—loses its simplicity.

We may strive mightily and still not achieve the results we desired or expected. Many of us did not get accepted to the college of our "choice." Many were passed over for promotion in spite of long hours at the office.

Older children may be experiencing, perhaps for the first time, the sometimes unfair gap between effort and achievement. They may work hard and not get the credit they deserve. In class, they can raise their hands with the right answers and the teacher calls on other students. Their efforts can be overlooked. They can study for a test and know all the answers, but then someone looks over their shoulder, copies their answers, and gets the same grade or even better. They can spend two hours working on a lesson that takes someone else 20 minutes. They can put in more effort than someone else and get a lower grade. None of these things is fair, and yet they happen.

Our job as parents is to prepare our children to make hard efforts, and to keep making them, even and especially when they get discouraged.

---

## "It's Unfair, It's Unfair!"

Jessica has been a conscientious and enthusiastic student from the start. She's one of those kids who plays soccer, plays in the band, seems to enjoy school, and gives her work her best shot. Not all subjects come naturally to her, but she plugs away.

One day she came home from school with tears streaming down her face. "It's not fair. It's not fair. I don't want to go back to school anymore. My teacher's not fair. I do all my homework and what does it matter."

"What happened?" asked her mother.

"I'll tell you," said Jessica, "but you won't be able to help me."

"Let's hear it anyway, honey."

So, Jessica told her mother what happened in class that day. The class had been assigned a short paper to write about a school subject that really interested them and why it did. Jessica felt that she was prepared. Her friend, Ann, said she wasn't. Ann sits next to Jessica in class.

What happened, according to Jessica, is that Ann ended up with a better grade on the paper than Jessica and the teacher praised Ann in class. What's worse is that the teacher called Jessica aside after class and remarked that there were many similarities between her paper and Ann's.

Jessica was humiliated and angry and she stalked out of the room. Ann had cheated and gotten away with it. Jessica had worked hard and had nothing to show for it. She was really upset.

## How Can Something Like This Happen?

*Life, as the old saying goes, can be unfair. Unfairness happens for lots of different reasons.*

*Sometimes what happened can be based on a plain old misunderstanding. Usually, this is easy to explain, easy to correct. But sometimes what happened to you is caused by someone, yes, it can even be a friend, who didn't play fair.*

*The rules for playing a fair game are pretty clear. When you hit a foul ball, it's foul. When it comes to schoolwork, playing fair means doing your own work and taking the consequences for whether you've studied or not. Getting answers from someone else on the sly is cheating. That's not fair.*

It might be that your friend really did play fair and had studied and she really didn't look at your paper after all. She may well have deserved the better grade. Some kids like to say that they didn't study so that if they get a poor grade, they can explain it away and pretend it doesn't matter. If they get a good grade, so much the better for them because it looks as if it comes without effort.

But it might be true that your friend didn't play by the rules and she did look on your paper and somehow managed to come up with a better grade.

What we have to do is find out what actually happened.

## What Can I Do About It?

There are some ways to try to get to the bottom of this problem:

> Talk with your friend and ask what happened.
> Talk with the teacher and share the problem.
> Ask for a meeting with your friend and the teacher.

Probably you will think of some more. These are not easy choices. So, you want to think about the pluses and minuses of these actions in advance.

For example, will your friend feel hurt? or betrayed? By turning her in you may risk losing her friendship. Will the teacher think this might be "sour grapes" on your part? You need to think about their reactions before you decide to ask for a meeting. But, that doesn't mean you shouldn't do it.

## Will You Take Care of This for Me?

I would if I could . . . but this is your situation and it's best handled by you.

This is your friend, it's your assignment, it's your classroom, and your teacher will want to hear from you and will listen to you more than to me.

I can help by talking with you before you go to your friend or your teacher and hear you out. It will help to talk it through with me. It gives you practice. I may respond in some of the same ways they might. It will give you the chance to think about better ways to present the situation.

**Reminder:** *Even outgoing children can become shy and insecure about talking with their teachers. It can be very helpful (and takes nothing away from the child) to send a note to the teacher saying, "There is something important that my child needs to discuss with you." Teachers welcome and need this information from parents.* ■

## It Doesn't Matter, Anyway

*Yes it does. You care about your friend and want to continue to be her friend. If you don't find out what happened, you may not be able to trust her again. If she really did cheat, she has a problem and needs to work on it. You could well be doing her a favor.*

*You care about your work in school and want the recognition and grade you deserve. And your teacher needs to know if there is a cheating problem in class. Plus, it's very important for you to get experience in dealing with complicated situations like this.*

*That's why you can't just walk away from dealing with this situation. I am very proud of you and will be with you the whole way.*

**Reminder:** *This situation is similar to other kinds of tough situations that children can find themselves in. They may see classmates shoplifting, getting into fights, drinking, and using drugs.*

*Peer pressure to be "cool" is intense. So as not to appear to be a "goody-goody," children may want to avoid the situation altogether and turn the other way. Yet, more and more, the message from parents and from school has got to be that children need help and encouragement to face these complicated problems, and that they affect the entire learning environment.* ■

## What Can I Do to Keep This from Happening Again?

*There are some easy changes you can make. You can be sure that you are the only one who can see your paper. And you can ask for your seat to be changed. That might help, but mostly you have to put across this message.*

*You need to let your friends know that you expect them to do their own work. There are times when you will be cooperating on an assignment, but when it's an individual task, they need to do their own studying. That does not mean you don't like them. It means that those are the rules you play by. Keeping to those and helping when you can will gain you the respect that makes all the difference.*

## You Never Had These Problems

*I am not so sure. It is true that there is more you have to learn today. And that means more pressure. But, kids were kids even in my time, and I thought my classes were hard. And I liked some subjects more than others, just as you do.*

*While I liked some of my teachers, I didn't like all of them. And there were kids who cheated in my classes and there were kids who were smarter than I was and kids who were not as smart. I had some hard times and some funny times in school. One of these days, I'd love to tell you about them. Just ask me.*

**Stop:** *This could be a great opportunity to share a brief, true story about a funny or not-really-so-funny incident that happened to you when you were around the same age as your child.*

*You may also want to return to the story of Jessica and recap what you both think Jessica should do and will do.* ∎

## Talking Together: What's the Plan?

People work differently, and our children need to understand this. Mostly, they need to try to understand how they work best. Share some of your own secrets. Talk together with your child about how you get yourself ready to work and how you move through a project.

- Under what conditions do you work best? Do you need quiet or can you work in the midst of noise? Do you need a long lead time or can you work quickly and under deadlines?
- Do you need your own special place for work? What materials do you need? What advance preparation, if any, do you have to do?
- Do you move step-by-step through a project, from beginning to end, or do you start in the middle and work forward or backward?

Invite your children to think about their own methods for tackling their assignments.

- What do they do to get ready?
- How different is their approach for shorter and longer assignments?

Probably the toughest challenge for students is to find ways to organize their approach to their work. Share with your children how you tackle this. Ideally, we model for our children a basic system that can work for them as they study for school. It doesn't have to be fancy. It means that we show them how to keep track of their assignments. We show them the beauty of manila folders to keep the notes of ideas as they think about long-range assignments. And we take time to practice with them dividing up a big assignment, such as a research paper, into parts. The sharing and talk are really very important. They help to start grown-up conversations about work and how it gets done.

## Doing Together: Making the To-Do List

Children, as well as adults, can be overwhelmed with so many things they have to do that it's possible not to know where to start.

"The Longest Journey Begins with a Single Step." So, the first thing to do is find a way to take that step. Trying to figure just what that step is can also be hard to do. Here is one way to get started.

Begin by listing in any order that comes to you the things that you have to do. For a parent, it could be grocery shopping, work for the job, crafts for the holidays, preparations for a move. The same goes for your child. For the child, the list might consist of homework assignments, gifts to get, TV and movies to watch, friends to call, and so on.

To add some teamwork to this *effort*, say each of the things on your to-do list out loud to your partner, who writes the items for the other person. Try to keep your list to no more than 10.

Don't worry that you have not picked the first thing to do. That comes later. Now you each have a list and the things to do on it are in any which-way order.

Study your own lists and make a decision: Which three things need to be done before any other things on the list? Star those on each list. Now, you are ready to prioritize: You and your children will mark *1*, *2*, and *3* next to the most important items. Your child will notice that some of the things can be done almost together and that some efforts have a spillover effect onto another item. Move through the rest of your list, putting numbers next to each of the remaining items.

Children participating in this process build a sense of how to figure out what has to be done and find a way to take that first step.

# The Adult Connection

## Effort

## *Whose Homework Is It, Anyway?*

At a recent meeting of parents in the suburbs of Washington, D.C., the topic was preadolescent children. The discussion hit all the hot buttons about the dangers of peer pressure, money, sex, drugs; but when the topic of homework came up, the meeting really came alive.

> *"My child gets too much homework."*
> *"My child doesn't get enough."*
>
> *"My child asks me for help all the time."*
> *"My child never asks for help."*
>
> *"The teacher doesn't give enough guidance. My child has to try to figure it out all by herself."*
> *"The teacher gives too much guidance. There is not an ounce of creativity in the lessons."*
>
> *"I help my child with his homework a lot."*
> *"I never help. Am I supposed to?"*

The questions continued. The confusion and concern were evident. Homework is still a problem.

It was really all about the role of the parent when it comes to home-work. When it comes to children's homework, here is one area in which I often have to urge concerned parents to make *less* effort, not more.

Why . . . because too many times the child's homework and its prob-lems become the parent's problem. It's not just nagging to get children to do their work: It can spill over into the parent's doing the child's work.

The temptations are great: We want our children to succeed. We want them to get great grades. We worry that other parents are helping their children and we are not. The competition is fierce: The spots at the top are limited. We can often do homework faster and better than our children . . . at least until we get to the upper grades.

So, why not help, what's the harm. . . . A lot!

What starts with good intentions often ends with bad results. The grades may be fine, for a while, but children are getting the wrong message and that harm can last a very long time. The message is this: "If it's too hard for you, honey, just let Mom or Dad help or even do it for you."

At the recent conference at which homework was discussed, I kept saying, "Remember it's your child's homework, not yours." It was a message some parents really did not want to hear. This was clear in the comments around the room, until one mother stood up to report on the experience of her younger brother, now 30.

Tom, she said, was a bright, but very lazy student. He went to a good and demanding school.

All through high school, Mom and Dad basically did most of Tom's homework and Tom's take-home tests. Tom was bright enough so that he usually made it through the in-school tests, though he did not shine as he did on his homework.

When it came time for college applications, Mom and Dad stepped in to help. They filled out the forms, wrote the essays, and mailed the applications. Yes, Tom did get into the college of their choice, a very good school, too.

Tom went off to college, but he was not able to take his parents with him. When Tom got homework at college, he finally had to do it him-self. It didn't take long for Tom to end up on academic probation. Eventually, Tom had to withdraw from college. According to his sister, Tom is still having lots of trouble finding himself and what he can do, on his own.

Did his parents help Tom or hurt him? His sister has no doubts.

That's why, she explained, she does not do her child's homework. As for Tom, there may have been other factors involved, but the help he received from his parents really turned out not to be help at all.

## When Are You Doing Too Much?

The best advice I can give is to think about homework in the same way you think about sports activities in which your child participates. Do you go out on the field to catch the baseball? Do you tackle the opposing players? . . .

And keep remembering to talk with your child about the real pleasures of *effort* so that your child can say with pride about homework, "I did it!"

# Reading Together:
# Effort

## Books for Younger Children

*Little Red Hen* retold & illustrated by Paul Galdone. Seabury, 1973.
  Since her lazy friends are unwilling to help, the Little Red Hen plants, harvests, grinds the wheat, and finally makes a cake which her friends are all too eager to eat.

  • Compare the efforts of the Little Red Hen and those of her friends. Why was the Little Red Hen's reward worth the effort she put into it?

*Old Man & His Door* by Gary Soto. Illustrated by Joe Cepeda. Putnam, 1996.
  Misunderstanding his wife's instructions, with great effort and ingenuity, an old man sets out for a party carrying his door—which proves useful to many along the way.

  • What did the old man think while struggling to carry the door to the party? How did efforts benefit those he met along the way?

*Where Are You Going, Manyoni?* by Catherine Stock. Morrow, 1993.
  Walking the distance to her school, a child living near the Limpopo River in Zimbabwe sees many animals along the way.

  • Why was it important for Manyoni to travel to school each day? How will her effort be rewarded?

## Books for Older Children

*A Chair for My Mother* by Vera Williams. Greenwillow, 1982.

A child, her mother, and her grandmother save dimes to buy a comfortable armchair after all of their furniture is destroyed in a fire. Mother will especially appreciate it when she returns home from her job as a waitress.

• Why are the family members willing to make the effort to buy a new armchair? How is the mother's effort reflected in the actions of Rosa and her grandmother?

*The Great Migration: An American Story* with paintings by Jacob Lawrence. HarperCollins, 1993.

A series of paintings and minimal text chronicle the journey of African Americans who, like the artist's family, left the rural South to find a better life in the industrial North.

• Why was this called the "Great Migration"? Why did it take such effort to move to the North? What obstacles did those who made the journey confront?

*Two Bad Ants* by Chris Van Allsburg. Houghton Mifflin, 1988.

Two young ants have dangerous adventures in a human world depicted from unusual perspectives. Only with great effort are they able to return to the safety of their colony.

• How did the ants overcome the obstacles they confronted? Beyond size, why were these obstacles so daunting?

# Responsibility

# Finding the Best in Ourselves

## The Power of Involvement

**W**HEN SHOULD CHILDREN LEARN about responsibility? The answer: almost from the "get-go." When that occurs is not on any chart. It falls in the crowded area of "doing the best we can."

Babies emerge helpless: We do almost everything for them. We all get used to it and that makes it doubly hard to know when to start asking them to do things for themselves.

Some parents with a number of children think back to their first child and remember that they didn't know how much their child was capable of. They didn't know what to expect, and they expected very little. With their second and third children, they report asking them to be responsible much earlier. And it works. Of course, the younger children have the models of their older siblings. They also have more confident and experienced parents.

While there are no set rules for all children, here are some basic guidelines that can help:

- Ask children what they feel they are capable of doing. Try to match these ideas with what really needs to be done.
- Ask yourselves how mature your children appear to be. Can they handle what they are asking to tackle? If what they ask to do isn't

safe and/or you can make it safe (such as washing dishes standing on a stool), let your child do it.

● Don't expect a perfect job. If it has to be a perfect job and your child needs to practice at it before it can be done right, wait until there is time to provide this practice.

● Try not to redo your child's work. Remember to provide reasonable praise and to keep thinking about the somewhat more difficult responsibility that your child can move to.

● Think beyond the home for children's growing sense of responsibility, especially for children in the middle-to-upper elementary grades. Try to connect with local community-service agencies and churches for assignments open to young people.

Very young children seem to know the helpful powers of responsibility almost instinctively. They start out pleading: "Ask me to do it. Teach me to do it." Most of it centers on household tasks such as setting the table or feeding the dog or bringing in the newspapers. They have the urge to be responsible.

As children grow older, they seem to lose some of this urge, at least at home. They begin to ask: "Do I really have to do that? Can't you get someone else? Later, OK?" They are testing us. Do we mean it? They are telling us that they have other things on their mind besides what we tell them to do. Even while we grit our teeth, we know that it's part of growing up.

Teaching children to take care of themselves (brush teeth, make beds, pick up toys) is challenging, but tougher responsibilities are out there. Teaching children about truth and honesty is harder to teach than picking up clothes from the floor. We can tell if the floor is picked up but we can't always tell it the child is telling the truth. We have to "grow" a responsible child.

We teach responsibility about truth by expecting it and letting our children know we expect it. This is the responsibility structure that children need; it starts at home. This is what this chapter focuses on.

It's this structure of expectations about responsibility that helps build children's sense of self-respect. As we see what we are capable of doing, we are able to do more and gain a sense of appreciation not only for ourselves but for others. Self-respect is truly the cornerstone of achievement now and in the future.

Through the activities in this chapter . . .

- You are creating within children an understanding about how responsibility works, in everyday family life and in the wider world.
- You are helping children realize responsibilities both to themselves and to others and learn how responsibilities build connections between people.
- You are working with children to develop ways for remembering what has to be done.
- You are helping children gain practice in making responsible decisions, and in gathering information needed to make these decisions.

# Losing a Backpack and Finding the Truth

## (Younger Children)

## The Story of Susie

Susie loves her new, blue school backpack. She picked it out at the store herself. It cost more than the others, but she really wanted it. Susie has a record of misplacing things. That's why her parents were not sure about purchasing this expensive backpack for her. But Susie kept on asking and asking for it everyday until her parents finally said, "Okay, let's go buy it. Remember, you have to take care of it. Be sure not to lose it."

"I promise," said Susie. And she was good to her word, until . . . one day after gym class, she went to the shelf where she usually kept all of her things.

The backpack was not there. She searched and searched, retracing her steps back and forth from her classroom to the gym. She looked under her desk and in her cubby. She searched the playground and the lunchroom. She went to the Lost and Found. She asked everyone, "Did you see my blue backpack?" No one had seen it and it was nowhere to be found.

Susie worried the rest of the afternoon about what her parents would say. She worried that she would be punished. She worried about what to say and then she got an idea. Susie decided to make up a story about how her backpack was taken from her by a mean boy from the school down the block. Nobody could blame her then.

She felt bad about losing her backpack. She felt bad about making up something that was not really the truth. But she felt relieved that she had something to say to her parents.

## I Lose a Lot of Things, Don't I?

*People lose things for a variety of reasons. Sometimes adults lose things because we get to thinking about something else and absentmindedly put our glasses or keys in a certain place and forget where.*

*And that might be happening to you. Maybe your head is full of other ideas when you need to focus on remembering where you put your things. You might be like an absentminded professor.*

*Or maybe it's that you just don't take good enough care of your things. Sometimes I don't know which it is. It would make me angry to think that we bought you this new backpack and you put it down and simply forgot where you put it.*

## You Do Believe Me, Don't You?

*We believe you, and we need to know a bit more. It would be good if you could tell us more about the boy. Where were you when this boy came up to you? What did he look like? What did he say to you? How was he dressed? We need to know this so that he can be found.*

*We need more information before we go around accusing people. What more do you have to tell us?*

> **Reminder:** *Ideally, children need to feel free to tell their parents the truth—warts and all. Do children feel they have to lie to get out of possible trouble? These don't have to be big lies to start a pattern of lying.*

> *Do they have to say that they took back the library books on time so that they don't have to admit and be soundly scolded for taking them back a day late? Do they have to find someone else to blame so that they don't get all the blame*

*all the time, even for small things such as tracking in some mud or not clearing the table or even turning off the light?*

*Do our children have a sense that they can admit to problems and work together with us to find solutions for the future and be forgiven now? With this understanding, it will be easier to get to the truth, both for children and parents.* ■

## I Got So Scared!

*Did the boy scare you so much or were you scared that we would be angry? What scared you the most?*

*You have to understand that you are very precious to us and that things, no matter how expensive they are, are not as important as you are—and they are not as important as the truth.*

*We have responsibilities to each other and one of our biggest is to tell the truth always. That goes from us to you and from you to us.*

*Is there something more you want to tell us?*

## All Right. There Was No Mean Boy.

*What is most important right now is that you have realized your responsibility to the truth, to us, and most of all, to yourself. We know it took a lot of courage for you to get over your fear and to be honest.*

*Yes, you did promise not to lose your backpack and, yes, you did lose it. And yes, we are sorry that this happened. Together we have to find ways to help you know how to take care of your things and to know where you can leave them. And yes, you need to be more responsible about your things.*

*It makes us unhappy to think that we scared you so much about losing things that you were afraid to tell the truth. I hope that this doesn't happen again. I hope that you will always tell the truth and not be afraid.*

*What is more important than losing a backpack is finding that you can tell the truth no matter what. The truth is what makes it possible for us all to trust each other, and we have to be able to trust each other . . . no matter what.*

## What Are You Going to Do Now?

*What do you think we ought to do? You've already been punished by losing your backpack. If you had kept talking about the mean boy who took it away, we would have had to figure out a way to teach you how wrong that was.*

*Even if we could afford it, we're not going to buy a new backpack right away. You may want to save up for one. What we have to do now is think about finding ways to help you be more responsible, so that you know that you can take care of yourself and your things.*

**Stop:** *Take a look at* Doing Together: Responsibility Reminders *on page 115. These provide a menu of ways parents and children can choose to keep reminding each other about responsibilities. They help keep us focused without nagging.* ■

## Talking Together: Keeping Our Promises!

"I promise" may be the two most trust-building words in the language. We count on each other to make promises and, most of all, to live up to them. They are the contract for our responsibilities to one another.

This activity helps us give ourselves credit for living up to our promises. Promises don't have to be *big* in order to be important and build trust.

Think together about promises you have made to each other in the past day or, if memory serves, in the past week or even the past month.

As a parent, did you promise a certain dessert for supper and then lo and behold it appeared on the table? Did you promise a reading time before bed and it happened? Did you promise to be on time for the soccer game and you met your promise?

As a child, did you promise to do your homework without having to be nagged, and you did it? Did you promise to make your bed and did it? Did you promise to call Grandma and you did it?

You made promises and you met them. Give yourselves credit! Maybe you also made a promise or two that you did not meet. Those may well come up in the conversation. Try to keep on the positive, but for those promises that still need to be met, talk about what you will do next time to make sure that these promises are kept.

## Doing Together: Responsibility Reminders

What helps us keep focused on what we have to remember? Some folks may still rely on memory, but a growing number of us depend on various methods to keep on track with what has to be done and to garner ideas from the family on what to do next.

Responsibility Reminders come in a variety of styles. That allows us to pick the style that suits our own household.

**Box:** Create a box (like a suggestion box), only in this case you might call it *Our Reminder Box* or come up with a more creative name. In it can go notes for each person in the family—"Please remember to . . ."

**To-Do List:** Some children thrive on these lists. They especially enjoy crossing off the tasks as they are completed. The system need not be complicated—just a list of things to do. The most important ones can go right to the top. It's always helpful to have easier and harder tasks on the same list. In this way, at least some things are sure to be done.

**Just Plain Old Notes:** Keep plenty of note paper, pencils, and markers around the house. You never know when you might remember something. And you can send these notes to one another, leaving them on pillows, on the bathroom mirror, or any place and anywhere that is bound to get attention.

**Job Charts:** Young children especially like the kind of chart teachers use at school. There's the list of tasks to be done, accompanied by who's to do them. Children like seeing their name posted and feeling a sense of accomplishment from getting the job done.

Whichever Responsibility Reminder system you choose, keep it going a while to see how it works for the family. Feel free to tinker around with it until you find a system that works for you and that you can stick to.

# What Friends Are For

## (Older Children)

## The Story of Alan

Alan's friend Jimmy lives down the block. Both boys have gone to school together since kindergarten. They used to be very good friends, but lately, Jimmy has started hanging around with some other kids and Alan thinks he could be getting into trouble.

Alan is pretty close with his parents and they know Jimmy's family, too. One night at dinner, Alan started to talk to his parents regarding his concerns about Jimmy.

Jimmy used to get top grades in the class, but lately they are going down. Alan and Jimmy used to study together, but Jimmy doesn't call or come by anymore. Alan can see when Jimmy leaves school that he isn't carrying any books with him, and that he is with his other group of kids.

Alan says that he tries to talk with him, but Jimmy waves him away and says he will talk to him later, but he never does.

## Did I Do the Right Thing in Telling You About Jimmy?

*Yes, though it may feel funny. It may feel as if you are a "tattletale," but you have done the right thing. It shows that you care about Jimmy.*

*You are being a friend to Jimmy when you tell us about this. Loyalty means responsibility to our friends. It means helping, and not just being quiet.*

*We can help each other only when we know help is needed. It sounds as if Jimmy needs help. And it sounds as if his parents need to hear about this.*

## What Do You Think We Ought to Do?

*We have some choices. We can have a talk with Jimmy alone. Or we can talk with him and his parents. Or we can talk with his parents alone.*

*We can't say for sure that Jimmy is in trouble, because we don't know. We know for sure that his grades are going down and that he has left his old group of friends and that he isn't studying as much as he used to.*

*We have to learn more before we say too much. Maybe we can invite Jimmy and his family over for a picnic. This will give us a chance to talk in a friendly way and maybe that will put our minds at rest. We may learn that Jimmy is doing fine and that we don't really need to worry about him. Or, we may learn that he really is starting down the wrong road. In that case, it will be important to talk with him and with his parents.*

*People don't really want to hear difficult news. Even though we are doing this out of friendship and responsibility to Jimmy and his parents, we need to be careful not to hurt his feelings. We need to show that we care and that we want to help.*

## What Do You Think We Ought to Do First?

*Before we decide to do anything, it helps when we try to put ourselves in the other person's shoes.*

*What do we think Jimmy might want us to do first? Do we think he'd like us to talk to him before we talk to his parents? That seems reasonable to me.*

*And what about Jimmy's parents? If you were a parent and you had a child who might be on the verge of getting in trouble, what would you want from your friends?*

> **Stop:** *Take a minute to review the story of Jimmy and ask your child about what he would want you to do if he were Jimmy.* ■

## Do You Think Jimmy Wants Us to Do Anything?

*We can't get inside Jimmy's head. He is probably feeling confused. He may not even recognize it.*

*In some ways, it's very hard to be growing up these days. It seems as if kids used to be able to be "kids" a lot longer than they are today.*

*You probably wonder what I mean. It's this: There is just so much in the world today—more things to know, more things to do. All that sounds good, and really it is. But it is hard to make good choices.*

*Most grown-ups today did not even know about the dangerous consequences of choices that they were making. There was a lot less known about smoking and drugs when we were kids. There is a lot more crime on the streets now and violence coming at us through the media.*

*So, while Jimmy may not want us to do anything, he is making choices now that could get him into difficulty later. As his friends, we have to find ways to help.*

> **Reminder:** *Risk taking has become more risky. There is more real danger out there. Children today have to know a lot more about how to protect themselves. This is a burden of responsibility and choice-making at an early age that goes far beyond what most of us experienced. It is hard on children. It's hard on parents.* ■

# Do Grown-Ups Always Know How to Make the Right Choice?

*I wish I could say yes, but it's not that easy. What grown-ups have is more experience. That helps us in thinking things through and in having more chances to make good choices.*

*Today, there is more freedom in daily life. With this freedom comes responsibility.*

*And with freedom comes choice. That is the hard part. When other people make choices for us, there is less personal pressure. Pressure and choice are part of life. It helps when we talk about it. Let's keep talking. In that way, we will be helping each other with hard decisions.*

## Talking Together: Growing Up Responsible

Discuss with children some of the key differences between easier and harder decisions and between children's and adult responsibilities. Middle- to late-elementary years are an ideal time to put responsibility into perspective.

What Are Different Responsibilities in Children's and in Parents' Lives?

- For children, these include: living up to certain commitments such as completing homework and cleaning up after ourselves, doing what we say we are going to do.
- For parents, these include: living up to certain commitments such as doing work on the job, taking care of the family, doing what we say we are going to do.
- Do responsibilities we have help determine whether we are grown up?

How are parent and child responsibilities alike? How are they different? How do adults try to make responsible decisions?

**Stop:** *Share these thoughts with children. The experience of being grown up doesn't give all the right answers. The best we can do is call on the best within us. That means giving decisions a lot of serious thought and trying to weigh the options. It's almost like putting our choices on a scale. The scale is inside our heads. On one side go the reasons for making a certain choice. On the other, go the reasons for not making the choice. This gives us a better chance of making a responsible decision.* ■

## Doing Together: Choices People Make

We don't have to go far to find true stories about responsibility and irresponsibility. They jump at us daily from the newspapers and TV.

There are articles and features about people doing all kinds of irresponsible things (such as writing bad checks, driving carelessly, and causing accidents).

**Select three or four articles or TV features and talk together about the choices the people in these articles have made.**

What do you think went through their minds?
Did they weigh the possible consequences?
What made them think they were making good choices?

Together, you are figuring out what makes these people tick—about responsibility and more. Trying to understand others helps us to understand ourselves and to know more about what we might do when called upon to make some of these same choices.

# The Adult Connection

## Responsibility

## The Education Pledge

It would be so easy if we could just send children off to school and say, "Get educated."

Actually, we used to think precisely along those lines before we knew better. We used to think that the school could do it all . . . or almost all. Only through the research and experience of the last few decades have we learned how much children learn before school and after the school-day ends. We have learned that the home—all homes—are critically important educational institutions.

What we now know is this: When families are involved in their children's education, children do improved work in school and the schools they go to are improved.

This means that families have educational responsibilities that go beyond getting children fed and dressed for school. There has to be a learning environment at home that puts across in word and deed the importance of education, and schools have responsibilities in reaching out to families so that children have the benefit of an effective school/home learning partnership.

To create and sustain this effort, home and school have complementary responsibilities. Parents and teachers working together help each other live up to these commitments.

## From Home to School

**Major Message:**  I recognize that I have important responsibilities in helping my child achieve school success. Regardless of my own educational background, whether I am rich or poor, I know that I have strengths and I am ready to help my child.

**Home Environment:**  I will work with my child to prepare our home for learning—with a quiet, lighted study corner and limits on TV watching and telephone calls. We'll be organized for work with a calendar, bulletin board, clock, books and newspapers, bought or borrowed. We'll brighten this study corner with a plant, a picture, a colorful blotter, a new notebook. It will be my child's special place.

**Preparation for Learning:**  I will do my best to make sure that my child eats nutritious meals and snacks, sleeps enough, gets plenty of physical exercise, and knows how to keep safe, so that attention can be paid to the work or learning. I will work with my child to set up household routines, for meals, for study, for TV, and for friends, that provide structure and limits, so that schoolwork takes first priority over everything else.

**Discipline:**  I will work to put into place a discipline structure at home and to maintain consistent, effective discipline to ensure that my child learns appropriate behaviors, respect and tolerance for others . . . so that my child comes to school ready to learn with others and to function well in the classroom setting.

**Time with Child:**  I know that it doesn't take a lot of time to do a lot of good, and I intend to spend time with my child, even when there is hardly any time. We will talk together about what happens at school, at home, and on the job. We will do things together, from sharing chores to sharing our leisure. We will seek to share many happy experiences. Some of the best things in life are still free.

**Communication with School:**  I will want to know what is happening at school, and what is happening with my child. I will not be afraid to ask questions or to take a respectful yet proactive approach with my child's teachers and school administrators. But perhaps even more important, I will provide information for teachers about what is happening at home, about any family concerns that teachers need to know about.

**Pledge:**   I will let my child know through my words and deeds that education is important. And I will reinforce for my children my faith in their ability to pluck the fruits of the "learning tree," and encourage them always to do so.

## From School to Home

**Major Message:**   While in my classroom, your child will feel and be treated as special and important. I believe in every child's ability to learn and in every parent's ability to help.

**Classroom Environment:**   I will make the classroom inviting, attractive, and stimulating so that your child, at least on most days, will jump out of bed, eager to come to class.

**Preparation for Learning:**   I will expect that your child will come to school in clean clothes, having had enough sleep and having eaten a healthy breakfast. Snacks and bag lunches will be nutritious. Junk foods will not be sent to school. If there is a problem at home about providing these essentials, you will let me know so that I can work with you to seek help.

**Time with Child:**   For children to succeed in school, they need time with parents at home. I expect that you will spend time with your child reading, playing, and doing jobs together—so that your child feels the security and encouragement that it takes to learn.

**Discipline:**   I will expect your child to come to school with sufficient self-discipline to be able to work within a group, to exert self-control, to pay attention, and to show respect for teachers and for classmates representing a rich diversity of backgrounds.

**Communication with Home:**   I expect to hear from you throughout the year about your child's school progress, that you will attend parent-teacher conferences, that you will read messages sent from school, that you will keep asking how you can help at home, and that you will expect me to have specific suggestions.

**Pledge:** I am committed to the success of your child and to working with you as a partner to help your child succeed. We will keep each other informed about how we, as a team, can continue to foster your child's achievement.

> **Reminder:** *Families and teachers can do a lot, but only so much. It's up to our children to take the next steps . . . to meet their own responsibilities. There's an old joke about a mother carrying around a grown son. Bystanders comment, "poor boy can't walk." And the mother replies, "Sure he can, but thank goodness he doesn't have to." Children who have been helped to become responsible walk with pride on their own.* ∎

# Reading Together:
# Responsibility

## Books for Younger Children

*Jamaica's Find* by Juanita Havill. Illustrated by Anne O'Brien. Houghton Mifflin, 1986.

When a little girl takes home a stuffed animal she finds in the park, she must decide if she will try to locate its real owner.

• Why did Jamaica think she did the right thing with the toy she found? How did her mother help her decide what to do?

*Hunky Dory Found It* by Katie Evans. Illustrated by Janet Morgan Stoeke. Dutton, 1994.

A playful dog carries off all sorts of things—until his owner makes him return them.

• Why did Hunky Dory's girl make him return what he snitched? What did Hunky Dory's girl try to teach him about responsibility?

*Sam Who Never Forgets* by Eve Rice. Greenwillow, 1977.

In spite of the elephant's fear, Sam the zookeeper never forgets to feed the animals in his care.

• How could the animals count on Sam? Why did the elephant doubt him?

---

## Books for Older Children

*It Takes a Village* by Janet Cowen-Fletcher. Scholastic, 1993.
On market day in a small village in Benin, Yemi tries to watch her brother and learns that the entire village is watching out for him, too.

- What links the village merchants? Why do they care what happens to the little boy? How did Yemi feel when she discovered her little brother missing?

*Talking Eggs: A Folktale from the American South* by Robert San Souci. Illustrated by Jerry Pinkney. Dial, 1989.
Kind Blanche following the instructions of an old witch gains riches while her greedy sister makes fun of the old woman and is duly rewarded.

- How did Blanche honor her agreement with the old woman? Why were her actions more responsible than the way her sister acted?

*Train to Lulu's* by Elizabeth Fitzgerald Howard. Illustrated by Robert Casilla. Bradbury, 1988.
Two sister travel alone by train from Boston to their great-aunt Lulu's Baltimore home in this story based on the author's childhood.

- How do the girls feel traveling alone on such a long trip? How does the older girl reassure her younger sister? Describe the family's preparation for the girls' journey.

# Initiative

# Making Moves

## It's New . . . and It's Scary . . .

**W**HEN WE TALK ABOUT confidence and motivation (two MegaSkills closely related to Initiative), we talk about *having* them.

When we talk about *initiative*, we're talking about *taking* it. Initiative is what we *do*, it's action, based on our feelings of confidence, motivation, and hopefully common sense.

For a long time, we can go along without having to take very much initiative. Our lives are routine, we know what to expect most days, and we amble along doing what we always do.

It's when change comes into our lives that we have to call on our initiative. It's when as adults we go to a new job or move to a different city. It's when as children we move up in the grades or move to a new school.

The friends we've had, the routines we have taken for granted suddenly are different, and we have to exert initiative to make new friends, to get comfortable in new jobs and new schools.

Being shy can make new experiences harder. There are children who come up to us and without our asking they say, "Hello, my name is John. Who are you?" And there are the other kids, the majority, who have to be asked, sometimes more than once, "And what is your name?"

Most of the time shyness is not a big problem, but it does mean that we have to provide some help. It's like working to get over stage fright.

How do actors do it? They rehearse and they visualize the audience and the scene. The same strategies can help our children. They can rehearse the new situations in advance. It may not go exactly as planned, but there is a comfort in having a plan and having a sense of what might happen.

Among the more difficult experiences children face is when their families move and they have to go to a new school.

Having new teachers, making new friends, using new textbooks—these call for every bit of gumption, bravery, and courage children can muster. Here's where children have to show their initiative, and it's not easy.

Feeling like an outsider is always hard. But, it seems especially hard for children. Being different is *not* what children want to be.

Moving is especially hard on shy children. They tend to stand back, to worry more, and to have more fears about whether other people will like them. Children who are shy can be mistaken for being aloof and for being stuck up. In a new setting, being shy is a handicap . . . but it can be overcome.

Even when children don't move from school to school, they need initiative to move into the higher grades. It takes initiative to be assertive and optimistic. And these are qualities it takes to get the most out of schooling.

In this chapter, the younger child, Maria, is going to a new school in a new city and she's scared. The older child, Tamara, is moving from grade school to junior high. She is feeling pessimistic. To combat these down feelings, she and her parents use special initiative/optimism-building exercises.

Through the activities in this chapter . . .

- **You are helping children get practice identifying their own and others' initiative.**
- **You are building children's abilities to use initiative and learn why certain responses work better than others.**
- **You are helping your child get over the shyness barrier by easing the process of "plunging in." You are creating a sense of security in an insecure time.**
- **You are providing comfort and reassurance that your child can take initiative, maybe not all at once but in important small moves.**

# The New School

## (Younger Children)

## The Story of Maria

Maria is the youngest of three children. She is known as "the shy one." She is somewhat small for her age. She's shy about speaking up in class and usually waits to be asked to get into a game. Maria's family does not have a lot of money, and she wears a lot of hand-me-down clothes from her sisters.

Maria has been going to the same school since kindergarten. It's a small school and the teachers all know her and her family. Yet, she has not found it easy to make friends and to feel confident in class. She tries hard and her teachers know it, so she gets good school reports. Still, she doesn't have a lot of friends.

Finally, this year, Maria made two friends. She is beginning to feel more comfortable in school and her teacher has noticed that she is starting to raise her hand more and speak up in class.

Then her father told the family that they were going to move to a big city in the next state. He had an offer of a better job. Before Maria was entered in school, the family had moved twice. Her family knows what it means to change schools, and knowing Maria and how shy she is, they are worried about her.

Her mother decides to have a talk with Maria . . . to help her open up and talk about her fears and worries and to give her advice about what it takes and how to use initiative in her new school.

# Will "They" Like Me?

*Sure, who couldn't help loving you, Maria? We all love you, and we know you. One of the things we know is that you are shy, sometimes very shy. This can be a problem, because the kids at the new school won't know that.*

*Let me tell you what happened to me: When I went to my first new school, when I was your age, I was shy, too. At recess, I stood by myself at the side of the yard. At lunch, I sat down alone at a table away from the other kids. I thought I had to wait for other kids to come up to me: to invite me to play or to sit with them at lunch.*

*They didn't know that I was shy. Later, they told me that they thought I was stuck up and that I didn't want to be friends with them. All along, I wanted to be friends very much but I was too shy to say so or to go up to them.*

*My advice to you is this: Try not to stand back. Start getting started. Let's talk about some of the ways you can do this.*

> **Stop:** *Share a few ideas on how to reach out and start connecting with children in the new school:*
>
> *Ask for help. Don't pretend to know where a room is or what the assignment is if you don't know. There's a chance that some kids might make fun of the "new" kid, but there's a better chance you'll get good advice and talk with and meet classmates.*
>
> *Try hard to participate. It's all right to be quiet until you are ready to talk. Listen and be attentive. When someone says something funny or interesting, say so.*
>
> *Be willing and ready to talk. When someone asks about you, tell them where you came from and what it was like. If no one asks, ask some of the kids to tell you about themselves. Whether young or old, we like to talk about ourselves.* ■

## Will the Teacher Like Me?

*Why not? You're very likable.*

*Your teacher needs to get to know you. Teachers are very busy and sometimes it's easy to overlook a shy student like yourself. Very often, it's the kids who misbehave who get a lot of attention.*

*You want to be sure that the teacher knows what you are good at and what you like to do. You like to read and you like to write stories. Let the teacher know this. I'll try to help you find stories you've written at your old school so that you can take them in with you and show your new teacher. This isn't bragging. This is sharing, and good teachers want to know as much as possible about their students.*

## Will I Be Smart Enough?

*Probably yes, because you know that you are a good student and the school you've been going to is a good one.*

*Chances are, however, in the first few days, you may get the impression that everyone else is so much farther ahead. It's because they may use different books or that they've been on a different schedule.*

*Let me tell you what happened to me in first grade: I entered a new school about a month after the term started. The other kids were working in a book that I had not seen before. So at first, when they were talking about the book, I didn't know a thing and felt really out of it.*

*But, by listening carefully, I was able to figure out the story. By following along, I found that I really could read as well as the rest of the class. At first, however, it seemed very hard.*

*What you have to do is pay close attention. Ask for a seat as close up to the front of the room as possible. Keep your eyes and ears open.*

*Remember that the teacher is there to help you. If at first you don't want to ask your questions in the middle of the class, go up to the teachers, when the* class is over and ask them. Also, ask about any books or materials that the teacher thinks you ought to know about.

It's hard to be new. The teacher understands this and wants to help. But, you have to take the initiative to ask for help.

## Will I Be Alone a Lot?

Not if you take the initiative it takes to reach out to make friends. When the class goes out for recess and everyone joins in a game, join in, too. Don't wait to be asked.

When you go to the cafeteria, sit down with some of your classmates. Chances are, you will know if some kids are friendlier to you than others. Join in the conversation. Tell them where you're from, and ask them about themselves. Where do they live? How long have they been at this school? Ask them to tell you something that you need to know as a new student.

Some kids are really nice about wanting to make new friends and others are in small groups or cliques. They have put a fence around themselves. So, start with the group that seems more open.

If by chance you have made a mistake and the group you chose to sit with is rude to you, try not to treat it as if it's a major calamity. It's those kids. It's not you. Tomorrow, you'll sit with another group.

The same thing happened to me. I got shunned by the first group I tried to be friendly with at my last school. But, I kept on trying and eventually, I found the group that became my best friends.

## Will I Really Have Friends?

Sure you will. I know from my own experience how hard it is to leave your old friends. Now that you know from your old school that you can make friends, it won't be as hard to make new friends.

*Of course, you will keep in touch with your old friends. Maybe some day you will be able to visit each other. Mostly now, you have to think about new friends.*

*When I went to my last new school, I wanted to have new friends so much that I showed that I was just too eager. I kept asking kids to sit with me and play with me all the time. It was too much. Some of the kids thought something was wrong with me . . . that kept some of them away.*

*Try not to act pitiful the way I did. You'll have friends soon enough. Just try not to worry.*

## How Long Before I Am an Old Girl in My New School?

*It's hard to tell, but it will go a lot faster when you take initiative to get involved and to make friends and be part of the new school.*

*Some groups of kids and some schools are easier to "break into" than others. They are more used to having new kids come into class. Other schools are less used to it.*

*As a family, we will try to get involved with the school, and this makes it easier for all of us. We'll show up at school meetings and the parent-teacher conferences. We will volunteer to help with school activities. When the whole family gets involved, it makes it easier for the school to get to know the new students and to begin to treat us like "old timers."*

## Talking Together: Recognizing Our Initiative

It's important to recognize daily acts of initiative and give children credit for them. Take a few moments to talk about initiatives (the daily kind) both at school and at home.

Children show initiative at school by:

- raising their hands to give answers
- volunteering to do tasks such as washing the board

- distributing materials
- doing extra assignments

Encourage children to add other ideas. They know their class experience better than parents do.

Children show initiative at home by:

- making suggestions about family outings
- working alone and with others to get chores done
- offering to help without even having to be asked

Add ideas here that children may not recognize as initiative. This is a chance to identify and praise children's daily initiatives.

Lists like these provide both a reminder and a recognition of all we do. Keep track and keep adding to the list.

## Doing Together: Putting It Together

It takes initiative to do some of the most ordinary and necessary tasks of everyday life.

When we look at our desks and say, "That really needs straightening," it takes initiative to do it. When we check our closet and see shoes thrown every which way, it takes initiative to get them paired up again.

Children use initiative daily. In every home there is some place that is chronically messed up, a place that would work better if it were straightened up. Here's the opportunity to stop the dawdling and take the action.

The tool drawer?
The sewing chest?
The toy box?
The kitchen cupboards?
Any other place?

After you complete one task, move on through the house. Together with your child, pick at least one place in each room that could use picking up. Set a date and do it!

When children find things that go together and put them together, they are practicing what schools call "classification." These are exercises children have been doing since toddlerhood (remember those "shape sorters"). The home gets a well-ordered closet or drawer and children get important, basic experience in how to organize . . . a key skill for academic work.

# Actions That Make All the Difference

## (Older Children)

## The Story of Tamara

Tamara is a hardworking student. She has every right to feel good about herself. Instead, she usually puts herself down, and tends to assume, when talking about situations at school and at home, that the worst will happen.

Tamara is becoming an adolescent, but she is also becoming a pessimist. Because of her new attitude, she has trouble speaking up in class and standing up for herself. She is starting to say, "I don't know," when asked for her opinions.

Above all, she is dreading the big move to middle school, as she is convinced that things are going to work out badly . . . that she will get mean teachers, that the new kids from the other elementary schools in the community won't like her, that she doesn't have the right clothes, etc., etc.

Tamara comes to some of these pessimistic feelings "honestly." Both of her parents have worried a lot about over-building Tamara's expectations. They don't want her to be disappointed, even by life's normal setbacks. So, they tend to go the other direction: When they speak about the future, they qualify everything. This way, Tamara won't be disappointed.

What they don't realize is that Tamara is becoming increasingly reluctant to use her initiative. This is serious. Tamara needs initiative to work effectively in her new and more demanding school setting. She will need initiative all her life, to enter and succeed in every new situation she will encounter.

Tamara is like a lot of other kids. So we are going to try something different here. On the next few pages are some multiple-choice situations with optimistic and pessimistic responses. As you discuss each of the problem "scenes" that follow, keep thinking about and asking which response helps build initiative and keeps optimistic feelings alive, and why?

For each situation, you are encouraged to come up with your own responses. To make trading back and forth easier for children, the initiative-building responses are noted. But, you may come up with better ones yourselves.

## The Call That Didn't Get Returned

*Andrew left a telephone message for Karen to call him back. He spoke to Karen's mom and he was really nervous. This was the first time he had ever called a girl in his class. He wanted to find out the homework assignment but he also liked Karen. He told his parents that she didn't call him back. What do you think they said?*

**a.** She must be stuck up and rude.
**b.** Don't call her again.
**c.** Call to see if she got your message.
**d.** Your own response . . .

> **Stop:** C *should jump out as the obvious choice, but you might have come up with a more optimistic response for* d. *For each situation that follows, talk about the response choices with your child.* ■

## Why Does This Always Happen to Me?

*Mike was really looking forward to the class field trip. That morning he woke up with a fever and a cough. Mike has a tendency to get real sick when he doesn't take care of himself. His parents told him that he was too sick to go* to school. Mike was really disappointed. He told his brother that nothing good ever happens to him. What do you think his brother said?

**a.** Come on, Mike, stop feeling sorry for yourself.
**b.** You're right. You have all the rotten luck.
**c.** There will be another field trip and you'll be on it. You have to get better first.
**d.** Your own response . . .

(**Answer:** C is the Initiative Builder.)

## The Big, Bad B

*Julie was an excellent student and she usually got the top grades in the class. Today, as she carried her report card home, she was really upset. There in the middle of all of her As was a B. What would her parents say?*

**a.** What's wrong here? Why did you get this B?
**b.** You got a great report card. Congratulations!
**c.** That teacher must have it in for you.
**d.** Your own response . . .

(**Answer:** B is the Initiative Builder.)

## Getting Called On in School

*It seems as if the teacher never notices Jane. She raises her hand to answer questions, but the teacher always seems to call on someone else. Jane is getting discouraged and thinks the teacher does not like her. What do you think she ought to do?*

**a.** Talk to the teacher. Jane should let her know how she is feeling and ask for her advice.
**b.** Tell the teacher how angry she is and tell her she is never going to participate in class from now on.
**c.** Just stop raising her hand. The teacher will notice soon enough, and ask what's happening.
**d.** Your own response . . .

(**Answer:** A is the Initiative Builder.)

## Who Will Talk to Me?

*Tom has been invited to a party where he doesn't know anyone. He is worried about what will happen, whether anyone will be friendly, how he ought to behave, and whether he really ought to go or not. What advice should we give Tom and why?*

**a.** Don't go. No one will talk to you anyway.
**b.** Go and actively try to make some new friends.
**c.** Go and stand around. Someone will come up and talk to you eventually.
**d.** Your own response . . .

(**Answer:** B is the Initiative Builder.)

> **Reminder:** *We are always making choices about . . . what we wear, what we eat, how we behave. While it's good to be conscious about what we do, the danger rests in becoming too self-conscious.*

*Helping our children get into the habit of using their initiative often gives them the practice in doing, in making mistakes and not worrying about them too much. That keeps us able to keep on doing.* ■

## Talking Together: What and Where?

The world is filled with initiative. Check the newspaper, check the TV, and you find stories about people using their initiative.

Clip some of these stories, and talk together about them: What are these people doing?

* Setting off on a trip to outer space?
* Designing a new convention center?
* Starting a business?

Initiative has its dark side. Adults take initiative when they rob banks and when they hurt others. Children take initiative when they dare others to fight and do some stupid or harmful acts.

Spend some time preparing your child for this dark side of initiative. What do you do when a kid starts a fight? What do you do when you are dared to do something stupid?

Children need to know how to say "no" to dumb and cruel ideas. One of the best ways to teach this is to practice what to say and do when initiative turns ugly. Rehearsals and role-playing are among the best ways to prepare so that children aren't caught off guard.

## Doing Together: Getting Organized for Action

Many people have good ideas, but it takes more than an idea to move into action. You have to get yourself prepared. That takes initiative, and it takes organization.

One example is coming up with the idea to have a party. The idea is fine. But what do you have to do to make it happen?

Even if you are not actually planning a party right now, use it (or another idea you come up with) to get practice in getting organized and ready for action.

- When will it take place? Where?
- Who will be invited? Do we send invitations or call?
- Do we have a budget?
- What will we serve?
- How do we decorate?
- What entertainment will we plan?
- How do we divide up the tasks?
- How do we pay the bills?
- How can we cut costs?
- How do we have a lot of fun, safely?

One of the biggest organizational tasks adults face is when the household moves, when all the pots and pans and chairs and beds and linen, etc., have to get from one place to another.

To illustrate what's involved in this massive job, ask children to brainstorm with you the steps you would have to take. What would you do first? Second? Third? It's mind-boggling but it's a great example of what it takes to organize an initiative.

# The Adult Connection

## Initiative

## *New Home/New School*

Congratulations! You have just bought a new home, in a new area. But it's March, and there are still three months left to go in the school year. What should you do?

Conventional wisdom goes like this: If at all possible, wait to the end of the school year—especially if you are moving to a new city—and make your move so that children can start fresh in the new school at the beginning of the new term.

This may or may not be good advice. According to experienced parents who have moved children to new schools many times, it can be just as good, and maybe better, for children to "just plunge in" and not wait.

Their point is this: When the family moves to a new place in the summer, and the children don't have friends, and they're waiting for school to start, it can get more scary for them than it needs to be. Their fears have time to build.

Alternatively, starting in the middle of the school year, kids have no other choice than to just plunge right in and get started. They may feel strange at first, but in a very short time, they make friends, they keep up with the class, and it works faster and smoother than waiting. This means that maybe we really don't have to worry so much about children when they move to a new school.

Of course, it always depends on the child, on the new school itself (is it a welcoming place for new kids?), and on the family (is it providing the guidance and support that children need?).

It's important to learn about the school in advance. This helps you figure out if a move at midterm will work as well or better than a move at the end of the school year.

Visit the school, talk with the principal, meet some teachers if possible. Take your child with you.

Ask about the program of studies and the extracurricular program. Can clubs be joined in midyear? To what extent is the curriculum similar to or different from what your child is currently learning? At the secondary-school level, it is important to learn about the transfer of course credits.

Once at a new school, parents/caregivers have to use initiative, too. It's important to plunge right in, to get involved in school activities, to become part of the new school community. The school provides an important entry point to the new family's introduction to the community. It's around school events, conferences, socials, and sports that families come together and get to know one another. This is good, not just for the children in class, but for the whole family.

"Plunging in" is good advice even when we don't move our household. Adults take initiative when we take on new challenges . . . in their personal and/or professional lives. These range from exercise to gardening to learning a new language to computer classes to Internet training, and on and on.

It's important for children to see that the adults in their lives are still learning. Parents report that when they go back to school and talk with their children about what they are learning, their children take a renewed interest in their own studies. Parents and children find themselves studying together.

New starts can begin in the same home or in a home across the country. We make these special new moments in our lives that enable us to think about what we are doing, what we have accomplished, and then "plunge in" and start something new.

# Reading Together:
# Initiative

## Books for Younger Children

*Henry the Sailor Cat* by Mary Calhoun. Illustrated by Erick Ingraham. Morrow, 1994.
   A stowaway cat proves his worth as a sailor during a sudden storm.

   ● Why did Henry stow away on the sailboat? How did Henry's actions show his initiative?

*Shy Charles* by Rosemary Wells. Dial, 1988.
   Being painfully shy does not stop a young mouse from rescuing his babysitter in an emergency.

   ● How does Charles's behavior demonstrate his shyness? Why are his parents concerned about it? How does Charles react to being called a hero?

*Letter to Amy* by Ezra Jack Keats. Harper, 1968.
   Peter wants to invite Amy to his birthday part but he wants it to be a surprise.

   ● Why does Peter want to invite Amy to his party? How does his letter show Peter's initiative?

## Books for Older Children

*The Aunt in Our House* by Angela Johnson. Illustrated by David Soman.
Orchard, 1996.
   When the aunt comes to live with them, the entire family enjoys her
company and helps her forget about the home she lost.

   • How does the family help the aunt forget? Why do they care so
   deeply for the old lady?

*Cherries and Cherry Pits* by Vera Williams. Greenwillow, 1986.
   Bidemmi beautifies her neighborhood through her love of cherries,
her ability to see possibilities, and her artistic talent.

   • Why is Bidemmi concerned about making her neighborhood more
   attractive? How do cherries symbolize her actions?

*Miss Nelson Is Missing* by Harry Allard. Illustrated by James Marshall.
Houghton Mifflin, 1977.
   The kids in Room 207 take advantage of their teacher's good nature
until she disappears and they are faced with a vile substitute.

   • What did the kids do to make Miss Nelson so angry? How did she
   respond? How did Viola Swamp react to the kids' behavior?

# Perseverance

# Making Time

## Keeping at It

**P**ERSEVERANCE IS PROBABLY THE foremost factor in children's school success. It's mighty important all through life, but it's the key for doing well in school.

We can have all the MegaSkills, but unless we have perseverance, success in school and on the job will be hard to come by.

And when we see things begin to work because of our perseverance, we gain more confidence. It takes confidence and motivation to get started, but it takes perseverance to sustain the effort. It's a wondrous cycle.

Read about any scientist, any sports star, literary figure, or artist. They start with confidence, they have motivation, but all attest to how much they had to persevere.

Kids would be wise not to dream of being an overnight success.

Nobel prize–winners wait decades for their awards. Sports figures practice and practice . . . and maybe then have a chance at the major league. Musicians work and work before they get to Carnegie Hall.

There are very few overnight sensations.

Can we teach our children to persevere? Yes, but it is hard. Concentration spans are shorter now. Adults and children increasingly listen and think in sound bytes. Teaching perseverance is more important than ever.

Just because something takes a long time does not make it perseverance. To persevere may take time, but time itself is not the measuring stick of perseverance. Otherwise, the child and adult who watch six or more hours of TV a day would be considered outstanding perseverers.

Perseverance is the personal quality we bring to an activity. We stay at it until it is moving along, done, complete. We have a focus and singleness of purpose.

It's ideal when parents can be models of perseverance, taking on projects at home that children can watch being worked on and completed: Making a dress, creating a birdhouse, reading a book, making a holiday dinner.

Kids can have goals, too: They don't have to be momentous to be important . . . jogging five minutes every day, reading ten minutes every day. We work with our children as they get started, provide encouragement as they continue, we can chart their progress, and celebrate as the goal is reached.

From these achievements, children build their persevering abilities. They gain the satisfaction of having worked a project through to completion, to achieving a goal. And then you can move to the next goal and the next. These are stepping stones to greater achievement . . . and perhaps they are all the more sweet because of the work we have put into them. We take pride in what we have been able to accomplish!

Communications experts, whose job it is to put messages across, say that these days it takes eight times of telling the same story before respondents say, "I've heard of that." As we reach out to others, even as we talk with children, we need to remember how many competing messages are in the air. Those who repeatedly work to get their message across, through their perseverance will most likely ensure their message will be heard.

Through the activities in this chapter, you are:

- Building children's understanding of the meaning of perseverance and how it is reflected in their behavior.
- Helping children learn how to persevere.
- Explaining what teachers mean when they talk about concentration and finishing a task.
- Developing in children an appreciation for the pleasures of completing work.

# Into Everything
## at Once

### (Younger Children)

## The Story of Steven

Steven has trouble paying attention. It's as if he has an attention span of only a few seconds. For Steven, a minute seems like an hour.

To be able to pay attention, Steven has to be able to handle frustration and focus on the subject. His attention span has to expand.

Steven has always watched a lot of TV since he was a little boy. As a matter of fact, the TV set is always on at his house. Most weeknights, the family doesn't sit down to a meal together. Everyone comes into the kitchen at different times as they get home from work, practice, or school; even the adults tend to eat standing up, or eat quickly at the table while watching the evening news.

At school, Steven has real trouble listening. When he's asked to open a book, write in his journal, or write down what he's observed in a science experiment, he's the last one to do it, and the teacher has to repeat the directions. It's as if Steven is always thinking about something else.

When it comes time to do a worksheet, Steven may start it, but he rarely finishes. He gets easily distracted and often is seen looking out the window. Sometimes, he's at someone else's desk when he should be at his own, and he's the student whose name is called more than anyone else's.

Steven's behavior at home and at school is driving his family and teachers crazy. Perhaps it's driving Steven a little crazy, too. His actions seem to be sending out a message: Help me settle down and be able to concentrate and do my work. Help me know how to finish projects I start. Help me know how to persevere.

## Why Does the Teacher Pick on Me?

*Your teacher is trying to help you pay attention to the work that has to be done. She has called me and told me that you always seem to be jumping up or looking out the window, and that you don't complete your work.*

*She wants to be able to help you. And she has asked me to help, too. One thing she wants our family to do is spend more quiet time together.*

*She asked me about noise in the house and whether our TV set was on a lot. I told her, "Yes." She suggested that we choose programs in advance that we want to watch and turn the TV off when we're not watching. She also suggested that we spend some time every day reading together.*

*I promised that we would. Your teacher doesn't want to pick on you, but she can't let you continue to disrupt the class. She thinks that you are a smart boy. She wants you to do well in school. And, she expects us here at home to help you, too.*

## My Teacher Says I'm Impulsive. What Does That Mean?

*It means doing things fast without thinking about them first. At school, impulsive children jump up and run around the room. They don't bother to raise their hands before speaking in class. They want what they want when they want it, and they don't wait their turn. Is that you?*

*At home, impulsive children may switch from one TV channel to another, even while others are trying to watch a certain program. They may start all kinds of projects, but they don't finish very much. They can't seem to wait. They don't persevere. Could that be you?*

*Everybody is impulsive at some time or another. Even me, even your teacher. As we grow up, we learn to keep our impulses under more control. That's what you need to learn and what we're going to work on together.*

**Stop:** *Share with your child an impulsive act you may have done as a child or as an adult. It may give you both some important insights, as well as a lot of laughs.* ■

## The Teacher Says That I Complain a Lot

*It's true. You do. When you have to do a chore at home that you don't like, such as clearing the supper table, you might start by taking away one plate, but then you get to complaining and saying, "I don't want to do this anymore!"*

*And sometimes it seems like more work to get you to do something than to do it myself. That's why you get out of doing many of the chores you're supposed to do.*

*I have to start making sure that you really do what you have to do. I also have to stop listening to your excuses. Even if it's hard at first, and it will be, I will really be doing you a favor. You need to get into the habit of doing your work, and you'll be able to.*

## Do I Have to Finish Everything I Start?

*No, you don't. For example, you may be trying some food that you don't like. You don't have to finish it. At school and later on when you go to work, you will have assignments that you don't like. But, you will do them because they have to be done.*

*If you get lots of assignments that you have trouble finishing, it may be because you don't understand them; we can talk to the teacher about that. If it's a very long assignment, we will find ways to divide it so that you can do a little at a time. That's what people do when they have a big job. They do one step at a time, and pretty soon, the big job is not so big anymore.*

## I Want to Show I Can Persevere!

*That's a great idea! There are a number of projects you might want to work on. Pick your own assignment and your own goal. It doesn't have to be hard but it does have to show that you can stick to the job and get it done . . . even on days you don't really want to.*

*Let's think together about activities you can do that can last at least a whole week. For example, you can make your bed each day and put the spread neatly on it. You can set the table for supper every day. You can check the thermometer each morning and tell us what the weather is like. You can pick a book you want to read and spend at least fifteen minutes every day reading it.*

*You have lots of ideas, too. When you finish one week, I'll bet that you can go for two weeks and even longer with other assignments.*

## Talking Together: Doing What We Don't Want to Do

It's worth asking our children to think about how they already persevere. This includes schoolwork and more. It could be studying for the spelling test or the geography quiz. It could be sports, and it could be hobbies. It could be the time children saved money to buy a special item they really wanted. These questions will prompt children to remember the times that they really worked hard and, yes, the pleasure that they felt in completing and accomplishing something.

**Questions to think about—answers to share**

How do we know when we persevere?
Do others always know?
How do we make ourselves do things we don't want to do?
Sometimes perseverance feels like fun. Sometimes it feels like work.
What do we persevere at that is fun?
What do we persevere at that is work?
Can work and fun be the same thing?

## Doing Together: Listen/Then Do

Teachers in the early grades tell us that children have trouble listening. Perhaps it's because they have been bombarded by so much coming at them—from television, video, and computer; from the plethora of activity and choices available to them. This makes for children who are easily distracted.

Here's an easy activity that can help cut through the confusion. For this, all you need are listening ears.

Think of a real job at home that your child can do. It might be setting the table, taking out the garbage, bringing in the newspaper, hanging up clothes. Think of at least three or four instructions for this job. Ask your child to listen carefully as you say them. Example: "Take out four forks, four knives, and four spoons. Put these on the table in four place settings. Put the fork on the left, the knife and spoon on the right."

Let your child give you instructions to follow. They can be as easy or as complicated as you and your child want. In this way, you individualize this activity to suit your child.

As a special treat, organize an outdoor treasure hunt. Prepare a short list of items, such as a small stone, a branch, a green or red leaf. Give youngsters a paper bag for the collection. Turn this into a game by timing the minutes it takes to find the objects. Use this idea when you go shopping. At the store, your child can help you persevere to find the family's grocery items.

# *You Can Do Better!*

## (Older Children)

## *The Story of David*

All of David's teachers say: "David can do better." When the report cards come home, David's parents ask: "What does this mean? Are you doing the best you can?" David says, "Yes." And he believes it.

David doesn't understand that his teachers are reacting to what he is saying and doing in class. For example: When he is given a writing assignment, David usually asks, "How many sentences do we have to write?" When a reading assignment is given, David is the first to ask: "How many pages do we have to read?"

This wasn't so troublesome when David was younger and the expectations of his teacher and parents were not the same as they are today. Now that he is having to tackle longer and more challenging assignments, David is having a really hard time. He thinks he is doing the best he can, but that best is what worked in the early grades. It does not work now that he is being asked to be more and more responsible and persevering about his own learning.

David can't seem to be able to carry through on an assignment that has more than one part and that extends over a period of time. He recently was asked to do a term paper and he really didn't know where to begin: The thought of having to do so much on his own makes him very anxious. His parents noticed this and wondered how they could help.

David needs to take the leap into the kind of learning that is needed in the upper grades. He needs to build patience, to be able to tolerate the frustrations and the ambiguities of a longer assignment.

Let's listen in on David and his parents and how they work with him to help him become more grown up in his learning, how he can become a learner with perseverance. A term paper, even as much as we may dislike it, is an ideal way to practice handling assignments that take a long period of time.

## Why Do My Teachers Think I Don't Try Hard Enough?

*It's because you seem to be asking to do the very least you can do. When you ask a teacher, "How many sentences do I have to write?" the teacher is bound to think that you are not trying very hard. What would you think if you were the teacher?*

*You'd probably think that David is lazy, that he's looking for short cuts, that he doesn't want to go all out and show what he really can do.*

*I know that you are not really lazy because I see you work hard on some activities here at home. You practice your basketball over and over, you help me wash the car, you help your father mow the lawn, you take out the garbage. You're a big help here.*

*You don't tell me the car is too big to wash or that there is too much garbage to take out. You even like to read books, as long as they're not textbooks. You're the only one who figured out how to work the VCR and how to put the new bicycle together.*

*You know how to do a job and you do a very complete job. What you have to do now is transfer the idea of yourself as a person who can do the job . . . to your schoolwork. And you can . . .*

> **Stop:** *Spend a few minutes identifying the ways in which your child perseveres. Trade places. Ask your child to tell you how you persevere, too.* ∎

## What Do Teachers Mean by "You Can Do Better"?

Teachers say, "You can do better," all the time. Most of the time it's true. Students can do better when they try harder—when they read over their papers, when they study the material a second time, when they do more than the minimum that is asked of them, and so forth.

But sometimes a "you can do better" comment from teachers can be very discouraging. It raises the questions of what's good enough. Can a person always do better? When can we be pleased with what we do? That goes for adults on the job, too. If employers make the judgment that we can do better, they need to help us know how.

It seems to me that when a teacher says, "You can do better," you should ask, "How?" Tell me what I can do differently. Be specific. Give me examples. Help me know what I need to do. This is hard to do, but we have to do it.

## Why Do We Have Long Assignments, Anyway?

Long assignments, like a term paper, give us the practice we need to undertake a project that can only be completed over a period of time.

When you go to high school and college, and when you are working, you have to be able to see a long job through. In high school, you will have tests at the end of the semester that cover everything you learned during the whole term. In college, you will have long term papers to write. On the job, if you are a lawyer, for example, you may have to work months and years before you finish a case. If you're working on building a house, that, too, takes months and months.

We all need to know how to handle long assignments and we need the practice doing them.

## Can You Help with My Paper?

I will be glad to talk with you about the subject and read over your writing, maybe even suggest an idea or two. But, it's your paper and you have to write it.

After you do your first draft, revise it, and then do the second draft, you will feel so proud of yourself. That's the way I felt when I did long assignments. Even now I feel that way, whether it's a project here at home or one that I do at work.

Big projects feel almost impossible to tackle at first, but step-by-step they get done. Believe me, you will feel accomplishment and relief when it's complete . . . even when you groan all the way through it.

## I Have to Do a Second Draft?

Right. This is to help you get into the habit of improving your work. You need to be able to revise, edit, change, and improve all subjects you study and whatever job you do later on.

When you are a chef, for example, and you try out a new dish, it may or may not taste good. You have to go back in and fix it and make it better.

If you're a doctor and you give a patient a certain medicine and it doesn't work, you have to try a new medicine.

If you are a film actor or director, you will rehearse and then shoot the same scene over and over until you get it right.

If you're an inventor, you're always experimenting to improve whatever it is that you're designing.

It may be that the first draft of your paper will be so wonderful that nothing you can do will improve it. If so, it's remarkable and I will congratulate you. But, in the meantime, prepare yourself to do a second draft. Chances are, you will see or think of new ideas or ways to improve it that you missed earlier.

## Why Can't I Just Quit?

You can. But, the paper will still be due. Quitting before you finish will just mean that the project hangs over your head, and instead of completing it, it goes on longer and longer.

*Quitting means that you are not showing courage, and I don't think of you that way. I think of you as brave and strong. I remember the hard and brave things you do, and how you keep on trying. I remember when you first learned to ride your bike and how you kept on trying and trying until you did it. I remember how you help me when I sometimes get so tired that I feel discouraged. I remember how you come over to me, give me a big hug, and it makes me feel so much better. I know that you are not a quitter. I know that you can do your assignment and even more.*

## Talking Together: Extracurriculars

Very often, children show their capacity for perseverance in the area called "extracurriculars."

The student who has trouble in math class can often be an enthusiastic figurer of batting averages. The child who has trouble concentrating in class may be composing music in the evening.

These children need to have the strengths identified and praised so that they can see that they are capable of perseverance. In a very real sense, extracurricular activities are not extra at all. They are cocurriculars and deserve enormous respect for what they do and for what they show about children.

Children have opinions or ought to have opinions about extracurricular activities. Ask them.

Are extracurricular activities important?

When funding is short for schools, should extracurriculars be continued or cut?

If you were on the school board, which way would you vote? And why?

**Stop:** *Talk about these questions together. Talk with your child about the extracurricular activities you participated in at school and what you learned from them.* ■

## Doing Together: Family Exercise

New studies say that more and more American children are overweight (actually, the word is obese) and do not exercise enough. It's because, the studies report, we're all sitting around watching TV, and we're eating the wrong foods.

Here's a chance for everyone to stand up or lie down together and move those arms and legs and do a little exercise. Each day you'll do more and more and that's how you'll show your perseverance.

Talk together about a realistic exercise plan for the family. Think about these questions: Do we prefer to exercise alone or with others? Do we like to exercise indoors or outdoors? How much time can we spend on exercise daily? (It does have to be daily or at least a few times a week.)

List one or two exercises each person in the family agrees to do on a regular basis. Example: Jog fifteen minutes daily in front of the TV set. Take the stairs at the office instead of the elevator.

Think of what you do that may hurt your health: Smoking? Drinking? Not eating fresh fruits and vegetables? Can you name one "bad" thing you will try to stop?

Together make up a plan for a week-long exercise routine. Be sure to make it practical and realistic so that you give yourselves the chance to succeed. Figure out a reward if you both stick to the plan. Then plan for the next week, and the next.

Your perseverance together as an adult/child team will be doubly inspiring. You'll be keeping each other going.

# The Adult Connection

## Perseverance

## *Communicating from School to Home to School*

How many times do teachers call home to try to reach parents and get the answering machine or no answer? A lot.

How many times do parents try to contact teachers at school, without success? Often.

Teachers and parents have a hard time getting together, even for a brief phone call. It's called "Playing Phone Tag." The players quickly become tired and discouraged.

What can we do to insure we each get the time and attention we need from the other? It takes perseverance.

Here are four pieces of modest advice that come from my long experience as both a teacher trying to reach parents and a parent trying to reach teachers.

**1.** Try again. Call again. Don't worry about how many times you have tried to reach each other. Treat the new call as a first time.

**2.** Avoid the guilt-inducing words, "Why haven't you called me back?" Chances are you'll hear the usual excuses and they don't serve any purpose. You have reached each other—proceed from that point.

**3.** Remember that it really doesn't matter whose fault it is: Start with the message you want to give or the questions you need to ask. Forget about blaming each other. It doesn't help.

**4.** If a follow-up call is needed, agree on a date and time for when you are going to call each other again. Offer to be the one who makes the call. Put it on your calendar and be sure to remember to do it.

To get our message across these days, even to get our phone calls returned, takes more perseverance than ever before. With so much information coming at us all the time, many of us feel inundated, and rightly so.

Teachers and parents, ideally, should be communicating enough with each other so that reports from the school shouldn't come as a surprise.

With a learning contract and a set of goals—mutually agreed upon by student, parent, and teacher—everyone will be able to know in advance how well or how poorly a student is proceeding and, most of all, what help the student needs to do better . . . long before the report cards come out. Models of these contracts (or compacts) are available for review through the U.S. Department of Education: 1-800-USA-LEARN.

Parents need to be warned a long time in advance before the bad grade goes out. There are phone calls, the interim reports, and the homework papers that need to go back and forth.

The good news is that more and more schools are persevering to reach families. And vice-versa, news about an impending crisis at home should not, if at all possible, come as a surprise to the school. Keeping each other informed as we need to be . . . takes patience. It takes perseverance. It takes time. And, it's worth it.

# Reading Together:
# Perseverance

## Books for Younger Children

*Farmer Duck* by Martin Waddell. Illustrated by Helen Oxenbury, Candlewick, 1991.
Despite his fatigue, a kind, hardworking duck continues to keep the farm running smoothly for a fat, lazy farmer until the rest of the animals conspire to chase the farmer away.

* Why does duck continue to work so hard? What did "moo," "baa," and "cluck" mean?

*The Little Engine That Could* by Walter Piper. Platt & Monk, 1976.
When the other engines refuse, the Little Blue Engine tries to pull a stranded train full of toys and good food over the mountain in this now classic story.

* Why did the Little Blue Engine try to pull the train when the other bigger engines refused? What was her reward when she finally succeeded?

*Uncle Jed's Barber Shop* by Margaree King Mitchell. Illustrated by James Ransome. Simon & Schuster, 1993.
Despite setbacks and obstacles, Sarah Jean's Uncle Jed—the only Af-

rican American barber in the county—pursues his dream of saving enough money to open his own barber shop.

- What would have happened if Uncle Jed had given up his dream? What did Sarah Jean learn from Uncle Jed's perseverance?

## Books for Older Children

*At the Crossroads* by Rachel Isadora. Greenwillow, 1991.
South African children gather to wait for their fathers who have been away working in the mines.

- Why do the children continue to wait at the crossroads even when it appears that their fathers are not coming? Describe the reunion between the fathers and their children.

*Brave Irene* by William Steig. Farrar, Straus, Giroux, 1986.
Overcoming fierce weather and great obstacles, Irene successfully delivers the dress made by her poor, hardworking mother to the Duchess.

- Why was it so important for Irene to deliver the dress? What were Irene's heroic characteristics?

*The Farolitos of Christmas* by Rudolfo Anaya. Illustrated by Edward Gonzales. Hyperion, 1995.
With her father away fighting in World War II and her grandfather too ill to make *luminaria*, Luz helps create *farolitos*, little lanterns, for their Christmas celebration.

- How does Luz's creativity help her persevere during a difficult time? How do the *farolitos* symbolize Luz's success?

# Caring

# Showing That We Care

## Teaching Caring

**C**HILDREN ARE BORN WITH basic self-needs, but they are also "carers." Studies show that even infants respond sympathetically when they see those they care about in distress.

When I got the news that my father died, my daughter, a toddler, saw my tears, didn't say anything, put her hand in mine, rubbed my arm, put her head on my lap, and started crying herself. She did not know what had happened, but she did know that her mother was crying.

It's within home and school life that caring attitudes and behaviors are nurtured. This nurturing is important because caring feelings can dry up and shrivel. It's hard for caring to thrive in atmospheres filled with anger and where caring is not encouraged.

There is a kind of mixed message about caring. We want children "hard" enough to stand up for themselves, to withstand and overcome the blows and stresses of the world. Yet, our children need to be "soft" enough to feel deeply and to express their feelings of love and involvement with others.

How do we strike the balance between hard and soft? It would be nice to be able to think that our children's early abilities as carers continue and grow, just like that. But, as children grow older and live in the wider world, which provides lots of examples of lack of caring . . . it becomes more and more important to find ways to preserve our chil-

---

dren's abilities as caring individuals. We teach children when they are young to share their toys. It follows that we need to continue to teach our children how to share and how to care as they grow older. Caring builds on caring. When we feel cared about and cared for, we are able to be more caring.

School in general has not been known as a caring place. Instead, it's supposed to be hard, rigorous, academic . . . not soft and emotional. And yet, it is in school where so many of our emotions are displayed, practiced, built, and destroyed.

That's why we have to start looking at school in a new way . . . as a place to nurture a wide variety of our intelligences, including our caring abilities. It's very doable. It's just that we have not paid sufficient attention to this critical need for caring and feeling cared about.

In this chapter, the school is an important takeoff point for helping younger children show and know how to care for others. For older children, who tend to look so grown-up and self-sufficient, this chapter focuses on ways to show them how much they continue to be cared about, not just at home but at school, too.

Tommy, the younger child, has been asked by his teacher to care for a new boy in the class, Dmitri. Tommy is basically a very caring child and he is asked to be a friend, mentor, to the new boy. He is concerned about what the older kids might say. Will they laugh at him? Call him teacher's pet? He wishes he knew what to do. He feels torn and feels he can't get out of it.

As Robert, the older child, moves into early adolescence, he has been spending more of his time alone with his videos and the computer, in the school lab and in the library. Robert is at home alone after school, taking care of himself. His parents have been busy and Robert seems to have been keeping out of trouble. They thought everything was going along fine. It was not until they heard from Robert's teacher that they really started to pay attention to Robert.

Caring, like the other MegaSkills, needs practice. We get better at it. Young children learn to care for others by sharing . . . sharing their toys and their concern. Older children, particularly as they move into adolescence, continue to need to be cared for, not as much as when they were very young. They need caring, in a more grown-up way, keeping the attention of their parents and learning again and again they are loved and lovable.

Through the activities in this chapter . . .

- You are finding ways to nurture your child's caring instincts.
- You are helping children overcome reluctance to be concerned about others.
- You are helping children gain pleasure that comes from giving rather then just receiving.
- You are finding more ways to let your children know that you care about them and that they are worthy of love and caring . . . no matter what.

The story of Robert (older child) provides a look inside a parent-teacher conference in which adults try to solve a problem about caring. This conference is an example of how teachers and parents can focus on problem-solving strategies together . . . to help each other and their student/child.

# The New Boy

## (Younger Children)

### The Story of Tommy and Dmitri

Tommy has lots of spunk and lots of friends. He is the one who's usually the first picked for a team, and kids just naturally seem to like him.

Probably that's why his teacher picked him for a special assignment. It's causing Tommy a lot of concern and he wishes he could get out of it. The assignment is that Tommy has been asked by his teacher to be a friend to the new boy in the class. She called it being a "mentor."

Tommy's problem is that the new boy is new not just to the class, but to this country. His name is Dmitri. He dresses funny. He speaks funny. He is very shy. He hardly speaks English. The other boys make fun of him, and they laugh behind his back.

The teacher wants to help Dmitri adjust to the class and to become part of the group. She's picked Tommy to help because he is really "in the group."

Tommy has nothing against Dmitri. He doesn't know him and he hasn't really thought much about the problems Dmitri is having . . . nothing personal. All he wants rights now is to get out of the assignment.

## Do I Have to Do It?

*No, you don't. It's your decision. If you do decide not to, think about the reason for your decision. Do you refuse because you:*

- *Think the other kids will make fun of you?*
- *Don't want to be bothered?*
- *Don't like this new boy?*
- *Don't want to feel responsible?*

*Maybe you have other reasons, but if you decide not to be Dmitri's special friend, you need to know, for yourself, why you don't want to do it.*

## Can I Say No?

*Sure, but there are consequences, just as in every decision. Your teacher may be disappointed and may think less of you. Maybe, and most important, it might affect how you think of yourself.*

*Even if your teacher didn't ask you, maybe you should have been thinking on your own about how you could help this new boy. Your decision is not so much about what the teacher wants. It's about you and about doing what's right.*

## What Do "Mentors" Do?

*Mentors teach. They don't do it through books and lectures. When you mentor your friend, you will be showing your feelings, your concern, and your caring. You're more like a counselor, an advisor.*

*You will be teaching through your actions and your words. At lunchtime recess you might say, "Join in the game." If Dmitri hasn't played the game before, you would show him how to do it. If he makes some mistakes, and he will, you won't laugh. Instead, you encourage him. You would say: "You can do it. I know you can. Let's practice together." That's mentoring. You would want someone to help you if you had to start all over in a new school.*

## Why Should I Do It?

*There's an old expression, that it's better to give than to receive.*

*We learn a lot when we give. It helps us feel better about ourselves. We feel that we are helping to make a difference.*

*This new kid is no dope. He's had experiences that you haven't had. He comes from another part of the world. He may know sports you don't know or games or foods, and what it is like to live in another country. He has something to offer you.*

*He may not end up being your best friend. But, what you are doing is making it possible for him to make friends and to share and give what he has.*

> **Stop:** *Tell about a time when you were surprised as you learned something from someone you didn't think had something to teach you. It might have been how to keep a baby from making a fuss in the supermarket or how to bat a ball so that it really moves or how to add a certain something to a recipe. These are little things that can make a big difference.* ■

## Can I Do a Good Job?

*The other kids like you and respect you, and if you show that you care about the new boy, the rest of the group is likely to go along.*

*This is not an easy assignment. Dmitri may not be so easy to be friendly with. He is new and scared. He comes from a country that has been at war. He may not be used to trusting new people. So, you may need to earn his trust.*

*Your teacher believes in you and I do, too. Here's a real chance to show how kind you really are.*

## They'll Make Fun of Me

*Maybe, maybe not. But, so what? It's hard, but you have to be your own person. Others aren't you and you aren't them. You are the one being asked to help Dmitri.*

*Your teacher picked you for a reason. Maybe she knew the other kids might make fun of the person asked to help Dmitri. Maybe she figured that you were caring and that you were strong. I think she's right!*

*If your friends do make fun of you at first, what will you say? Will you say the teacher made you do it or will you stand up for yourself and say that you think it is the right thing to do. I hope you will have the courage to stand up for what you are doing and think of it as a right decision that you are making.*

> **Reminder:** *Being made fun of is no fun . . . for anyone, but especially for children. It can't be dismissed lightly. Our children need our support in standing up for what is right, no matter what other people say. It can be helpful to try to rehearse in advance what we will say if and when the "making fun of" starts.*
>
> *Conflict resolution is a relatively new training being provided to children in a growing number of schools today. The idea is to help children learn how to deal with their anger and their problems in getting along with other children. The key ingredient is TALK . . . talking through little problems before they become big problems. Conflict resolution can take place not just in the classroom but in any home. That's why it is so important to take our children's concerns about other children and what they will think seriously.* ■

## Would You Do It?

*I would like to think that I would, but I have to admit that when I was your age, I really did not understand very much about caring about other people.*

*I loved my family and my friends, but I had a hard time thinking about how other people felt.*

*When I think back, I realize now that my friends and I must have hurt a lot of feelings. We made fun of kids who were fat. We made fun of kids with handicaps. We teased almost anybody who was different. I now understand how wrong it was to be so unkind. It is very important to treat others as you would have others treat you.*

*None of my teachers asked me to do what your teacher has asked you. Your teacher is giving you a chance to do some real good.*

**Stop:** *Talk about a time when you, like Tom in this story, got the opportunity to take care of someone else. What happened? What did you do and why?* ■

**Reminder:** *Can our children try to imagine what it would be like to have a handicap? Start with some key questions and let the conversation flow. Who do we know who has a handicap? Anyone in the family? Anyone at school? How do we treat that person? This kind of caring and understanding can be built . . . and it starts right at home.* ■

## *Talking Together: The Subject Is Caring*

Here are some starter questions between adult and child to prompt big thoughts about caring:

- What does it mean when we try to "put ourselves in someone else's shoes"?
- What does it mean to act selfishly? unselfishly? Do we know or have we heard of an unselfish person?
- How have we experienced others acting unselfishly and selfishly?
- What's so good about being nice?
- Are there really special returns that come from giving? If so, what are they? How have we experienced these in our own lives?

**Stop:** *What if your child were Tommy and he or she was asked to help a new classmate. What specific ideas can you both share? Would you invite the classmate home? Would you spend some weekend time with him? Would you consider inviting his family over for a snack or dinner? Talk together about what you both think would work.*

*What if the teacher had not asked Tommy to help? Would Tommy or someone else in the class (on his or her own) offer to help? What do you think and why?* ■

## Doing Together: Take Any Day

Gift giving provides an opportunity to think about what would make another person happy.

Think about making gifts at home. Is there someone you know for whom you would like to bake cookies, sew a potholder, or construct a model plane.

Think about the people you'd like to give gifts to and what would suit each person. Think of gifts that aren't "things." You might share a special skill of yours to help someone, or give someone the gift of your time.

Some of the best things between parent and child are still free! And some of the best and surprising things between brothers and sisters are the caring they can show toward each other.

For children, it might be: "I will play ball with my younger brother." "I will make my sister's bed." Siblings' caring starts at home.

**Reminder:** *Even young children can become involved with their larger community. Gift making and giving are ideal for stimulating this connection with the community. There are so many ways to start: At holiday times, donate toys and books for other children; help in neighborhood clean-up projects; sort household recyclable items; save money from weekly allowances to make donations with the family to worthy community, school, and church projects. We don't have to give a lot to have it mean a lot, and children can learn this very early.* ■

# Attention Must Be Paid

## (Older Children)

## The Story of Robert

Robert, an only child, has been a very responsible kid for a very long time. He would always do his homework, without being nagged. He got top grades. He seemed almost more mature than his parents. He just seemed to take care of himself so well. Up until Robert started fourth grade, he stayed everyday after school waiting for his parents to pick him up at the school child-care center.

Robert kept telling his parents that he really could take care of himself at home and that he shouldn't have to stay at the center with all the little kids. So, as soon as Robert entered the fourth grade, his parents said, "OK. You can come home by yourself after school but you have to stay safe, you have to lock the door and be by yourself until we get home."

Robert is now in the sixth grade. His parents have gotten used to Robert being their little man. While they care deeply about Robert, they don't seem to have very much time for him. They have gotten busier and busier. After all, he seems to be taking care of himself so well.

So, it came as quite a surprise to receive a phone call from Robert's teacher asking them to come for a conference. She briefly described a situation that happened in class earlier in the week. Robert's teacher had noticed his work was not going as well as usual. But, it was not until she called Robert over to have a little talk about his work, that she heard Robert say four words that cut right through to her heart: "Nobody cares about me."

Robert's teacher knew Robert's parents were concerned about him and involved with the school. Why did he feel this way? Here are the questions Robert's parents asked.

## What's Happening with Robert?

*It's hard to know everything that is happening. But what I see is a child who seems sad and who seems lonely. When I went to speak with him the other day, I told you that he said that no one cares about him. It's not true, but if that is how he feels, we have to do something about it.*

*Robert is the kind of kid who is easy to take for granted. We depend on him to do the right thing. So, we don't pay him too much attention. It's possible that he is getting the wrong message. He thinks we don't care . . . because we go along assuming that good-old Robert will keep on being good-old undemanding Robert.*

*But, he is growing up and he is coming into adolescence and he needs a new kind of attention from all of us. Robert has given us a wake-up call and we have to pay attention.*

## Is Robert Alone Too Much?

*Teachers are not therapists, but I can tell what I know about basic signs of depression. Experts tell us that we need to look for certain symptoms that last at least a period of weeks. They include:*

- *The blues, crankiness, angry outbursts, and general irritability throughout most of the day.*
- *Major changes and excessiveness in lots of areas: eating, sleeping habits, restlessness, fatigue, difficulty in concentrating and in making decisions, plus overall feelings of hopelessness.*

*Symptoms like these used to get shrugged off, but not anymore. Depression is being taken very seriously. You will want to check with a counselor to get additional advice on this. Our school guidance office can provide more infor-mation and referrals to counselors.*

## What Kinds of Activities at Home Will Really Help?

**More Time Together:** *Most of all, find ways to spend more time with Robert. He needs to know that you care about him and what he does and what he thinks. You've left him alone because you think he wants to be alone. But he is giving us a different message.*

**More to Do at Home:** *Keep thinking about how Robert can feel more involved at home. He's growing up and he needs responsibility at home. That actually makes him feel you care more about him, because you are involving him.*

*Try to look for small, short activities you can do together such as choosing a dessert for dinner or watching a certain TV program and then talking about it.*

*Robert needs to feel valued. He needs to feel he has a positive role to play in the household. Anything you can do to put across that message, in words and in actions, is important.*

**New Friends:** *Robert is so much into loner habits that it may take some time to move him along in this area. This isn't easy, but there is some help you can provide. For example, you can suggest having one person over for a pizza; then they can talk or play on the computer together. Or you can invite Robert to a movie or a fast-food restaurant if he brings along a friend.*

*You're moving slowly, not starting with a big party. Robert has to get to want other people around. He needs practice in initiating and sustaining relationships with kids his own age.*

**New Interests:** *It's not going to happen immediately. He didn't get into his solitary habits overnight. But we can all work step-by-step.*

*At school I plan to make special efforts to get Robert involved in group projects. I'll pair him with other students with similar interests and get them talking together. Perhaps they can plan a presentation for the class. I will work to get Robert talking with me and with classmates. That's the beginning. He has to feel needed and involved.*

**Reminder:** *In a sense we would like to keep our kids, kids. But they refuse to stay very young for very long. Kids like Robert aren't really kids anymore. They are almost young men and women and they need to relate to their parents in a new, more grown-up way. They need to be able to have, give, and take conversations; share hopes and dreams and worries and fears; hear from their parents; and bounce ideas around with them. That's the way they grow up strong. And that is really what we parents want for them. But, it doesn't happen just like that. They need our involvement and they need our attention.* ■

## What Can We Do First?

*Start where you are. Tell Robert how much you care. Then start to show him. Invite Robert along when you visit family and friends. Because he's been alone so much, you may need to talk him into it. He's got to feel it's important that he joins you.*

*Find someone, an uncle or neighbor, who is willing to come by to talk with Robert about a special hobby. It could be stamp collecting or biking or swimming.*

*Help Robert get into the habit of thinking about what he has to offer others. Talk about this. Be specific; for example, can he teach another person about computers?*

*Keep emphasizing that he can do it, that you believe in him. Everyone needs caring; we care for each other. It's not just a Robert thing.*

*And, let's touch base with each other regularly to see what's happening at school and at home. We are partners in working for and with Robert.*

**Stop:** *Think about your own experiences with parent-teacher conferences and how this one is different and similar. Think about how you can make your own future parent-teacher conferences even more helpful. Start with one thing—one word, one action—that you will do differently; one question you may not have asked before.* ∎

## Talking Together: Taking Charge of Anger

Here's a talk-together activity that can help sort things out . . . especially the potentially explosive feeling of anger.

**Think together about what makes you angry.**   People get angry for different reasons. Some people get angry when others take something from them. Others get angry when people don't listen.

"You take my record without asking me. You ask me over and over how to start the computer and you don't listen."

**Ask yourselves: What do we do when we get angry?**   Some people try to cool off before they speak. Others start fights. Some people scream. Some people don't say anything.

"You sulk for hours. You say you're not mad when you really are."

**How do you act when you get angry at a friend?**   Do you talk it over? Do you just stop seeing that friend? Ask yourselves: How can we handle anger in a positive problem-solving way?

"You don't tell what is bothering you. You keep it all inside and then you explode."

**Choose a favorite television program.**   Watch for situations that make people angry. What do they do? TV, while not a great source of positive examples, does provide lots of examples of what not to do.

"You see people using guns to settle their disputes, and knives, and bombs. Talking things over is not very dramatic, but it's the only thing that really works."

## Doing Together: The "Look" of Feelings

You don't have to be an actor to do this activity. Some people take to this like ducks take to water. Others need a little coaxing. This is basically acting with a purpose—to see ourselves and to see how we see others.

Ask children to start with their face to show these different emotions. They can add their whole body at any time. Do it right along with them. Take turns looking into a good-sized mirror. First alone, then together.

Try some of these feelings and add some of your own:

Happiness
Sadness
Anger
Boredom
Shock
Surprise
Peace
Confusion

Ask each other: Is this really what this feeling looks like? Do you experience any of these feelings more than others? Which ones do you find easier to portray? Harder? Why?

Look for signals from family members, friends, teachers when they're feeling these emotions. Pick a time when you felt especially happy and tell about it. Tell about a sad time, too. Did anyone notice? Recognizing how others feel and connecting with these feelings (empathy) is a key ingredient in caring.

# The Adult Connection

## Caring

## The Kind of Caring That Counts

The kind of caring that counts is not so much that it stifles our children . . . and not so little that it gives our children the idea that we don't care at all.

How do we strike this happy balance? With great difficulty and lots of trial and error.

When our children are young, we protect, we protect, we protect. When they start to grow older, we try to back away and sometimes we back away too far. The story of Robert is a good example. He looks as if he is doing all right, but down deep he is scared and needs greater involvement from his family. He doesn't need so much control that he can't grow up, but he does need continuing caring from his family and he does need to feel that he matters and that his family respects him.

There is no getting away from parental responsibility, especially today, when the world outside our door offers more choice—and more perils—than ever before. Parents are not able to control everything, but they can help children exert their own self-control.

What is it that children need in the form of caring and support?

- Nurturing and friendship: unconditional love and caring
- Standards, boundaries: clear understandings about rules, discipline, and consequences
- Guidance and expectations: help in knowing how to achieve

What opportunities do children need?

- Discussion of ideas, talk about experiences
- Participation in sports, art activities, and classes
- Membership in a group or network
- A chance to be of service to others

Some adults these days have been accused of caring so much about themselves that they have forgotten their responsibilities to their children. We're not talking about carpools and gifts of money. We're talking about the time and attention it takes to raise children and to show them that we care. Surveys of parents today are none too comforting. Many parents today believe that they are not nearly as sacrificing for their children, nor do they want to be, as their parents were with them. And yet, we want to do a good and even great job.

The good news is that we as adults aren't done growing. We may be as tall as we are ever going to be, but we are continually developing inside. Our children need to see this.

We need a lot of what our children need. To be sure, as adults we have outgrown some of a child's needs for boundaries, but we surely continue to need nurturing and friendship.

As adults, when we seek out the supports we need, we are role models for our children.

- When they see us reach out for friendship and make friends, they learn from us how to make friends.
- When they see us have high expectations for our work, they see how they can have expectations for themselves.

- When they see us contribute to the community, as involved people, they see themselves as people who care and have the capacity to use their caring to make things happen.

The reassuring news is that as we develop ourselves, our children come along with us, when we provide the kind of support they need.

# Reading Together:
# Caring

## Books for Younger Children

*Mama, Do You Love Me?* by Barbara Joose. Illustrated by Barbara Lavallee. Chronicle, 1991.

Translucent watercolors depict an Inuit child as she learns that her mother's love is unconditional.

- Why does the child question her mother's love? How does the mother show her love?

*The Purple Coat* by Amy Hest. Illustrated by Amy Schwartz. Four Winds, 1986.

Despite her mother's reminder about the usefulness of a navy blue coat, Gabby's grandfather, a tailor, makes her a beautiful purple coat.

- How did Gabby feel about her mother's concern for a coat's usefulness? Why did Grandpa make the purple coat?

*Wilfred Gordon Mcdonald Partridge* by Mem Fox. Illustrated by Julie Vivas. Kane Miller, 1985.

Wilfred Gordon, a young boy, helps an elderly neighbor, Miss Nancy, find the memories she has lost.

- Why does Wilfred Gordon care about Miss Nancy? How does he show his concern?

## Books for Older Children

*Chicken Sunday* by Patricia Polacco. Philomel, 1992.
To thank Miss Eula for her wonderful Sunday dinners, three children sell decorated Easter eggs to buy her a beautiful Easter hat.

● Why were the Sunday dinners so special for Miss Eula and the children? Why did the children work so hard to surprise Miss Eula?

*Jamaica Louise James* by Amy Hest. Illustrated by Sheila White Samton. Candlewick, 1996.
For her birthday, Jamaica Louise receives paints which she uses to surprise her grandmother and brighten the subway station where Grammy works.

● How do Jamaica's paintings represent the way she feels? Why was it important to Jamaica to give Grammy something special?

*Teammates* by Peter Golenbock. Illustrated by Paul Bacon. Harcourt Brace, 1990.
Jackie Robinson, the first African American Major League baseball player, experienced tremendous racial prejudice when he first joined the Brooklyn Dodgers. This handsomely illustrated book describes those experiences and the support Robinson received from white teammate Pee Wee Reese.

● Describe how Pee Wee Reese felt when he saw Robinson's struggle. How did Jackie Robinson show his concern for his teammates and the game of baseball?

# Teamwork

# The Hard Part of Teamwork

## The Team Experience

TEAMWORK—THE BUZZWORD OF the nineties. It's the hot managerial strategy: Rugged individualism is out, teamwork is in.

The thinking is this: In this super modern world tasks are more complex and there are more specialists. This means that to accomplish a complex task, specialists need to work together as team members. It makes sense. Many of us have heard this refrain so often that we know the words by now.

This teamwork idea can sound easy. But it can be mighty hard. Actually, teamwork can be more difficult in the schoolroom than it is beyond the school walls.

On the sports fields, in the orchestra hall, on the assembly lines, in the creation of a film . . . in many lines of work, we accept and know that we have to work in teams. It's the way it works and it's worked like this for a very long time. In the classroom, teamwork is not a tradition. In fact, it's a relatively new concept. Teachers and students aren't used to it, and families can have a hard time accepting it.

We put children in teams and yet continue to grade them as individuals. When teachers do try to grade children as a team, it's hard to know where the team ends and the individual begins, and who's responsible for what . . . making some children feel that they have been unfairly treated.

Then, there are children who want so much to be on a team and find that they can't get accepted by the group. This can be one of the greatest heartaches of a child's school experience. That's why teamwork, which is supposed to make things easier, can actually cause stress in the schoolroom in the short run.

In the long run, teamwork can enable children to learn more from one another to build a sense of identity with the larger group, and build children's respect for diversity. In short, learning teamwork can better prepare children for the real world of today and tomorrow.

This is the theory, the ideal. In reality, whether in the classroom or on the job, we cooperate and compete at the same time. That's, as they say, life! Adults know this pressure and, by and large, learn to handle it. Children can, too.

Children already function as members of a team. They are members of the family team, the class team, the school team. Whether they like it or not, they are partners with a large number of people. Their own experience tells them that partnership does not always run smoothly. Anyone in a family knows that.

Teamwork involves a lot more than trying to fit in and "be nice." There are complex behaviors that children can come to understand and handle.

In this chapter, Toni is worried about her place on the team, worried about letting the team down. At the same time, she feels put down by the team . . . because she's been a student who needs special help. She wants to be accepted, she wants to do well and make everyone else proud of her and her contributions to the team. She's worried that she won't be able to do it.

Jason is dealing with partners on a teamwork project who, he feels, are letting him down. There is a major grade riding on this project. The teacher will be grading the team as a group. Jason's partners don't seem to feel any urgency about the project. Jason is worried that his grade will suffer and he wishes he knew what to do.

Through the activities and conversations in this chapter:

- **You are talking about grades, about what they mean and what they don't mean.**
- **You are encouraging your children to talk to you openly about their feelings of self-worth, of being as good as the other kids.**

- You are talking together about getting along with others, about how to handle conflict.
- You are talking with children about ways to work with others to gain acceptance, without losing their own individuality.
- You are helping children learn how to be assertive in the best sense, standing up for their own rights without putting down others.

# The Team Doesn't Want Me!

## (Younger Children)

## The Story of Toni

Toni came home from school choking back tears. She slammed her backpack on the kitchen counter and, taking the steps two at a time, ran into her room and slammed the door shut. "They don't want me on the team. The other kids think I'm dumb."

Toni's mom had just gotten home from work. She was tired and really wanted some peace and quiet for a few minutes. But she could see that Toni was upset. So, they sat down together on the sofa. Toni, with tears in her eyes, told her what happened at school.

Toni told how the teacher divided the class into teams to do a project on dinosaurs. Toni described how she was put into a team with a lot of smart kids in class. "We are supposed to work together on this project. But after we met in our group for the first meeting, the other kids told me that I wasn't smart enough really to help. They told me that they didn't want to be graded down or have to go slow because of me. I know that they didn't want me on the team, but they had to take me."

Toni has had trouble learning to read. She's not been able to concentrate well. One of the teachers at the school told her mom that Toni had a learning disability, but it wasn't so severe that she could not be in a regular class.

Instead, Toni goes to the Resource Room for extra help. She works with the reading teacher and she's making progress. But, it does take

Toni longer to read the material and to finish her assignments in the regular class. And sometimes Toni doesn't know the answers right away. But, it's not because she didn't try. She can hear the kids holding back giggles.

When Toni does know the answers, she gets so excited, she jumps up and down and calls out for the teacher to call on her. The kids laugh at her about that, too.

Toni is always one of the last children to be picked for anything at recess. Usually the teacher has to assign her to a team. But this doesn't bother Toni too much: Nobody gets grades at recess.

But now, Toni is being asked to work on an in-class team project that is going to be graded. Now it will matter. The other kids on the team told Toni they wish she had been assigned elsewhere. They know they can't change that. Instead they tell Toni that she can hang around but that she doesn't have to do anything. They'll do the project without her. But don't worry, they say, "We'll put your name on it with ours."

Toni knows that she is supposed to do her share of the real work, and she wants to. She tells her mom that she wants to prove that she can do it, but she doesn't want to get the other kids into trouble. She wants to fit in.

## How Can I Make Them Want Me?

*They don't have to want you, but they do have to respect you. Whether they want you or not, they've got you.*

*Without crying and without anger . . . just straight on, you need to let them know that you expect to be on the team and that you will be on the team no matter what.*

*Just because you are a different kind of learner does not mean that you can't contribute to a good project. And you will, whether they like it or not.*

*It's not easy to stand up for yourself like this, but it's good practice and learning to do this on your own will let you know how strong you really are.*

**Reminder:** *Take a few minutes to talk about respect . . . what we expect for ourselves and from others. We build our self-respect and worth, and even young children can have a conscious appreciation of their own standards. (For example: "I don't lie. I don't cheat. I am a good friend.") We should expect not to be put down. We need a sense of our own strengths and abilities.*

*Just as we are asked to respect the differences of others (in this case the "smart kids"), so should we expect these others to respect our differences. We start by not putting ourselves down.*

*Everyone has something important to contribute, and this is the attitude of self-respect that makes it possible for others to respect us.* ■

## Will You Talk to the Teacher for Me?

*Yes, and that might be a good idea. But the teacher has to promise to let you try to work this out for yourself. You're not a crybaby: You are a strong little girl.*

*If I go charging into the classroom and tell the teacher, she'd talk to those kids and make them do right . . . this time. But the next time, when you get put into a group and the group doesn't want you, you'll come home crying again rather than stand up for yourself. And we'd have to repeat the whole thing all over again.*

*What the teacher needs to know is that getting good grades is making the class a little crazy. It's getting in the way of their being fair and kind. It's destroying the whole idea of being on a team. I think she needs to know that. She probably doesn't even realize that it's happening.*

## Should I Just Do What They Want?

*No, you shouldn't. It's not good for you and it's also not good for the team, not good for what you have all been assigned to do—together.*

*There are kids and adults who seem to enjoy teasing and bullying others. When they do it, we try to walk away and we wish they would stop. Most of the time, it does stop when we don't pay attention. But, other times it goes on and on. It's hard but we have to stand up for ourselves, not by teasing and bullying back. That only seems to make things worse. We can walk away, and when it doesn't stop, we should ask for help from the teacher. It might mean having to change our team or change our seat to get out of the line of fire. But it also means that these children who are growing mean get to talk to grown-ups who can help them stop what they are doing.*

**Stop:** *Take a few moments together to practice what to say, what to do when your child is being teased and bullied. Take turns pretending to be the bully and to be the one who is bullied. What are some better ways to handle the situation? Try them out. Just as our children learn about and practice dialing 911 in cases of emergency, they can learn and practice how to react in cases of being bullied.* ■

**Reminder:** *One of the best ways to defuse angry situations is to use humor, to make fun of ourselves without putting ourselves down. We always seem to think of what we wished we had said hours later. For example: When we get teased about what we are wearing, it would help the situation to say, "Oh, you think these clothes are ugly. You should have seen what I was wearing yesterday." Or, "If you think that was a dumb answer, you should have heard what I said* *yesterday." Having this kind of response ready-to-use when needed can be very helpful . . . for adults, of course, but even for children.* ■

## I'm Not As Smart As They Are

*Different people have different smarts. You are smart in ways I am not smart and I am smart in other ways. The same goes for the kids in your class.*

*Some kids can learn math but they can't figure out music. Some kids can look at a word and know how to spell it immediately. Others have to spell it over and over. We all have different ways of learning. We are all special in different ways. We do things differently. We think differently. This is part of the excitement and diversity of the world. Some of us eat our cake first and save the frosting. Others eat both at the same time. Still others eat the frosting first.*

*We don't have to be super-talented or a genius to learn well. It's nice to be a genius but we can't count on it, so we have to use the gifts we have. We can't expect to be like everyone else and we don't need to be, either. The world would be a much less interesting place. The important thing is that we have the freedom to grow, to start from where we are and to keep on going.*

> **Stop:** *Name a few of your child's special qualities or abilities. Then trade places. Ask your child to name some of yours. You both deserve to hear good words and to feel the pleasure of appreciating your own specialness.* ■

## Can I Get Them to Like Me?

*Maybe yes, maybe no. Right now they think that you are someone who can be pushed around. When you stand up for yourself, they will see you in a new way and maybe that will make them like you.*

*But, try not to worry so much about them liking you. Ask whether you like them. It's all right not to like them, even if they are the most popular kids in the class. Right now, you have every right not to like them. They are treating you badly and unfairly. And that has to stop.*

## I Want to Be on the Team

*You do and you deserve to be. These children are unkind and uncaring and deserve to be punished. I could tell the teacher and she could give them a talking to.*

*But it would really be better if you could stand up to them and not let them bully you.*

*We'll talk together about what you can say to them. They may not get any nicer, but they'll know that they can't put you down.*

## Talking Together: Working As a Team

Teamwork is about getting along with others, sharing with others, and yet keeping our own individuality.

Children want to be on the team. They need playmates. They need teammates. Not everyone has to be picked as the most popular in the class, but we do need to be "picked" in some way.

How can we help (and not just feel bad) when our children come to us crying: "The other kids don't want to play with me!"

Here are some basics children need to know:

- Show the other children you are a team player. Let them know you care about them and about the team, and not just about yourself.
- Let them see that you are not selfish. Volunteer to play a position on the team others don't want. Share a toy you have. Show them that you are neither a baby nor a show-off.
- Don't keep apologizing for mistakes or when you miss the ball. Just say, "I'll do better next time. I'll practice." Show them that you have self-respect and that you intend to keep at it.
- And keep at it, not just for one day but for as long as it takes to let the kids know that you are a good sport and that you are willing to work very hard to be a part of the team.

## Doing Together: Special and Different

The world, even our own little world, is made up of lots of differences. All we have to do is look around us to see old and young; men and boys; women and girls; religious, racial, ethnic diversity . . . on our streets, in our schools, next door, right at home.

Differences need to be understood as natural, not as scary. It's worth taking a moment to think about, to look around, even to make a count of differences we see.

Start right at home, then move to the block and to the school and neighborhood:

- How many older people do we know? (This gets tricky. Your child's view of old may put their parents into the rocking chair.)
- How many children live around us? What are their ages?
- Do we know people of different races? of different religions? different ethnicities? How many different languages do we hear?
- Where did our own grandparents come from? (In America, we are all immigrants.) America is a nation of teamwork: different people working together.

Add more survey questions of your own. Your children will start identifying differences that may well surprise you.

Think of this exercise as a way to help children gain a greater sense of the growing diversity of the world and a feeling for how special and different we all are—something worthy of celebration.

# My Team Is Letting Me Down!

## (Older Children)

## The Story of Jason

Jason is in a sixth-grade classroom where the teacher really likes team projects. Jason likes them all right. But some of the students aren't so keen on them. They want to work with their own friends . . . if they are willing to do the assignments at all.

This new team project is really high stakes . . . the teacher has said that the grade on this project could be as much as one-third of the marking period grade. Jason is nervous about it. He is conscientious and he's heard that the grades he gets this term will affect what class he's placed in next year.

The teacher usually puts teams together. He tends to put a good student in with one who needs added support. Jason, who is a top student, usually finds himself leading the teams he's on, getting the others to cooperate. Most of the time, it works out even if Jason does end up doing more than some of the others. He hasn't really minded, until now.

Jason is assigned to work with three classmates on a project about what kinds of books and materials students in the "sixth grade of tomorrow" will be using. Jason is excited about the subject: He's collecting information about the Internet and the World Wide Web.

His teammates are slow to get going and Jason is worried that the whole project will be sloppy and late . . . and his own grade will suffer as a result.

Jason has never faced this kind of problem. When he nudges his team to get going, they tell him that if he really wants to do this work, he should do it himself.

Jason knows that his teacher does not want to hear excuses. He believes that the class needs the experience of working in teams and that the students need to work out their problems on their own.

Jason's been trying, but so far not much is working. Every day that goes by means less time for completing the project. He's getting more and more nervous and today he seems more discouraged then ever.

## What Can I Say to These Kids?

*You can encourage them. You can tell them how much they are needed and how important the assignment is. That may or may not work. They may have made up their minds not to do what you ask them to do.*

*This is a tough situation. You are the designated leader and your team members don't seem to want to listen and perform as team members. And it happens on the job with adults, too.*

*Sometimes kids don't realize how much they are really needed. Focus on what has to be done and not on whether you all like each other. That is not as important as the assignment and what each of you has to do to get the assignment done.*

*There are three other students on the team. It may be that one or two really want to do the assignment. You may need to talk with each member separately.*

*Remember that the task of a leader is to inspire and to help motivate the team into action. Think of yourself as a coach . . . think of what you will say to your players to help them do their best. Think of how you can help build their team spirit. It's hard but it's worth trying.*

## I Want to Get Off the Team

*The first thing that we need to do is try to find out more. You need to meet with the teacher. And if necessary, I will meet with her. Or we can both go together.*

## What Can I Say to the Teacher?

*You can tell him what's happening and you can tell him how much you are trying to get the assignment done.*

*He may say, "No excuses." He may even think you are being a bit of a tattletale. But when you present the facts of the situation without whining or feeling sorry for yourself, chances are, he will listen and hopefully try to make some changes.*

*He may talk to your team or suggest that you move to another team. Or he may think it's better for you to see this through. He may not realize how unhappy you are and how much this is affecting your own attitudes. As you speak with him, talk about this and remember to try to do it in a calm way.*

> **Reminder:** *When we send our children to have a talk with the teacher, encourage them—especially when they're talking about other students—not to put down the other kids and not to focus on grades alone. By and large, good advice when trying to work with schools is not to make children's grades the center of our conversations. Focus on the learning involved.* ■

## The Other Kids Say I'm Not Cool

*That is hard to take. This is what peer pressure is about. Peers, kids your own age, talk you into doing what they are doing or what they think is right or "cool."*

*You have to try to be as strong inside as you can be, knowing what's right for you and not for everyone else.*

## I Don't Like School Anymore

*You're discouraged, and, frankly, I don't blame you. But this will pass and you're going to work this out. It's possible, and I hope it doesn't happen, but you may be in situations like this in the future. You may be on a job doing the best you can and not getting support, recognition, praise, or a raise. It happens and it's not pleasant.*

*In situations like this, we have to keep our own heads, recognize our own strengths, and not be dependent on those who don't really know us or who don't care very much about us. We have to try to carry good feelings about ourselves in our own hearts. We have to be strong, just as you have to try to be strong now.*

## I Feel Bad When I Get a Bad Grade

*You want to achieve and you want to do well. That's wonderful, and we admire you. But you need to know that we will love you even if you get a bad grade. Your value is not based on your grades. We want you to work hard and do the best you can, but you need to know that you are very special no matter what.*

*This situation is especially frustrating. Despite your best personal efforts, you feel dragged down by others. This happens in real life beyond school, too. While we are going to do the best we can to turn this situation around, it may turn out that you will learn a lot by working through this problem. This will be very important for you in the upper grades and later on beyond school.*

> **Stop:** *Share with your child a situation in which you have had to work with others who did not feel the same way you did about the work, and tell about the kind of team building you had to do in order to get the job done. Not all of these stories have happy endings. The point is that we have to retain our optimism even when, especially when, situations are tough.* ■

## Talking Together: Teams and Gangs

Today's violent gangs are a far cry from the pals who gathered together as in "Our Gang." Both emerged from adolescent needs for friendship and support . . . but today's gangs, especially in urban centers, often

---

come together for acts of violence and criminal behavior. We may have to join teams but we don't have to join gangs. Kids need to know this.

Doing what the others do is the same for lots of other activities, from what to wear to what to eat to the dangerous choices about sexual behavior and using drugs.

The pressure on children, especially young adolescents, is extraordinary to do what *they* are doing, to be "cool." Our children need to know what to say when faced with this pressure. Moreover, they need the practice of saying it, of feeling comfortable with their own words.

Discuss with your child:

- Why do you think kids join gangs?
- Do you know anyone who is in a gang?
- If someone invited you to join their gang, what would you say? If you would say Yes, why? If you would say No, why?

Try to extend the conversation with additional back-and-forth questions and answers. And remember to listen even more than talk.

It's easier to talk about "Just Say No" than it is to actually say it. That's why it's so important to help children say it in their own way.

## Doing Together: Solo or Team

We are all, in many ways, team players. Take a moment together, adult and child, to list the ways in which you now work as members of a team:

**On the Job:** Am I working with others on a project at the office or plant?

**At Home:** When do I work together as part of a team at home?

**At School:** When do I work as a team member in school?

You can jot down your ideas on a chart similar to the one on the following page. It helps collect your thoughts about how you work— on your own and as a team member.

| Home | | School | | Job | |
|---|---|---|---|---|---|
| **Solo** | **Team** | **Solo** | **Team** | **Solo** | **Team** |
| Hobbies Homework | Cleaning the house | Workbook assignments | Sports | Reports | Meetings |

There are assignments we are asked to take that we don't really want to do, like playing outfield on the team when we'd rather be at first base. Because we are team players, we do it.

Make sure children understand that everybody gets into situations in which we have to work with people we don't really like. But, we have to get the job done, so we work together.

# The Adult Connection

## Teamwork

## *Parent and Teacher Stress*

It's not a secret that stress comes to school and goes home from school.

- The child who suffers disappointment about something that happens in school goes home angry and frustrated.
- The youngster who comes to school from home where parents are arguing sits in the classroom in a cloud of worry.

There is no way to keep our lives at home and in school totally separate. It works the same way when adults bring worries from the job home and bring home worries to the job.

The difference in the home-school relationship is that it's children carrying with them the situations from home that cause stress, including illness, divorce, and all the problems humans are heir to. A school can't put families back together, but teachers can play a significant role in helping a child of a family in trouble make it through difficult times. Vice versa, a family can't change a lot in a classroom, but can do a lot to ensure that their child comes to school ready to learn and eager to participate.

So-called small things make a big difference: We don't do these alone. We make these observations and take these actions as part of the parent-teacher team.

**Watching for Signs of Stress:**   We can be alert to the first signs: troubles in eating and sleeping, acting out (temper tantrums, screaming fits), acting in (not talking much at all, not wanting to be with others), and having trouble getting along with friends.

**Listening Hard:**   We can try to respond without giving a lecture. Just being there is vital. This is why there is so much concern about making time for children.

**Not Expecting Everything to Go Perfectly:**   We need to tell children that mistakes are inevitable, that we will forgive theirs, if they forgive ours. What makes stress more stressful is that we feel so unsure, not knowing what to expect.

**Getting as "Together" as Possible:**   This does not mean a tight schedule. What it means is getting things together, having a semblance of a schedule so that children feel more security. Children need reassurance that even while there is pain, things can get better.

Among the more challenging and more common stressful situations for children and parents is divorce. When experienced single parents give advice to newly single parents, for example, it goes something like this.

- **Organizing Home Life:** Organize daily home life and routines so that they are as constant and continuing as possible. Try to provide children with a sense of stability in an unstable time.

  Be as specific about the future as you can. Tell children where they will live, where their other parent will live, and how visits will be arranged. Follow certain basic rules. Maintain authority.
- **Informing the School:** Notify the school office of changes in marital status. Ask that the child's report cards and records also be sent to the noncustodial parent. Let the school know of any changes in address, telephone number, or job so that you may always be reached. Be sure this information is complete.

  Set up a parent-teacher conference. Try to be as honest as you can about what is happening to the family. Don't predict terrible behavior you might expect your child to develop. Let teachers know you will work closely with them to solve any problems.
- **Getting Support from Others:** Feeling overwhelmed and alone is one of the first obstacles parents and their children under stress

must deal with. It's hard, very hard, to think about getting organized, while feeling hurt and shaken. That's why it's so important to connect with others, to continue or start to build a support network. Use the school as a community resource center. Encourage the PTA to set programs that are useful for single and working parents on topics such as meeting the demands of home and job life. Ask the principal about organizing support groups for single parents.

Joining together with others is rewarding not only to parents, but also to children. As one mother commented: "Going to events at school has made it easier for my kids. They see other kids at these family activities and they're going through the same things, and they're surviving and having fun, so it looks like we will, too."

> **Reminder:** *We may not be able to banish stress, but we can battle it. That's the strength of parents and teachers teaming together.* ■

# Reading Together:
# Teamwork

## Books for Younger Children

*So Much* by Trish Cooke. Illustrated by Helen Oxenbury. Candlewick, 1994.
Although everyone loves the baby "so much!", the family gathers to joyfully celebrate his father's birthday.

- When is a family like a team? How do they work together to make a fabulous party for Daddy?

*Swimmy* by Leo Lionni. Pantheon, 1963.
Swimmy organizes a school of fish to unite them against common enemies in the sea.

- How does Swimmy organize the school of fish into a team? How are Swimmy's differences useful to the team?

*Zinnea and Dot* by Lisa Campbell Ernst. Viking, 1992.
Zinnea and Dot, self-satisfied hens who bicker constantly, lay aside their differences to protect a prime egg from a marauding fox.

- How do Zinnea and Dot become a team? How does the newly formed team successfully protect the prime specimen?

## Books for Older Children

*Anansi the Spider* by Gerald McDermott, Holt, Rinehart & Winston, 1972.

Each of Father Anansi's six sons use their unique talent to save their father in this boldly illustrated folktale from the Ashanti people of West Africa.

● Was any one son's contribution more important than another's? Why or why not? When did Anansi and his sons function best as a team? Why did Nyame decide to keep the great globe of light?

*Baseball Saved Us* by Ken Mochizuki. Illustrated by Dom Lee. Lee & Low, 1993.

During World War II, a Japanese American boy learns to play baseball when he and his family are forced to live in an internment camp, an ability that helps him even after the war.

● How does teamwork lessen the misery of the camp? How does the boy's skill at baseball help him become a member of the team in school after the war?

*Music, Music for Everyone* by Vera Williams. Greenwillow, 1984.

Rosa plays her accordion with her friends in the Oak Street band and earns money to help with expenses while her grandmother is sick.

● How is the band similar to Rosa's family? How do their skills compliment each other?

# Common Sense

# Getting into the Habit of "Knowing Better"

**W**E WANT OUR CHILDREN to have common sense. We say: "Use your common sense" as if we expect to see it hanging around waiting to be used. No such luck.

That's because common sense is really a form of self-discipline. Children are not born disciplined. They have to learn it, and it's taught by example and by practice.

At its core, common sense is about having a sense of how to regulate ourselves, how to avoid excessiveness, how to use our best judgment. It's about crossing a street safely, buying or not buying an expensive jacket, turning down drugs . . . all the common and not-so-common decisions of daily life.

Common sense helps us learn what is important and what is not. It puts us on the road to wisdom. It works on smaller things than wisdom does; it's daily, it's practical. Without it we get into lots of trouble.

How do we learn to use our common sense? Mostly, we get into situations that demand it. And sometimes we manage to use good sense and other times we don't. The preschooler pulling a temper tantrum in the supermarket is not using common sense: it's all the more reason the parent has to. The little one who pushes so hard to put a toy together that it breaks is not using common sense. On the other hand, the child who really doesn't want to write a thank-you for a gift but does it anyway is using common sense and being courteous, too.

Practice in using common sense is not easy to come by. That's because as parents, our instinct is to use common sense for our children. This often means that we make the choices for our children . . . protecting them from the consequences of their not using common sense. Not only that, there are times we think for them and put words into their mouths. When children come home after something has gone wrong in school, we may tell them what happened without even waiting for them to tell us. When we ask, "What do you think you can do about it?" we sometimes answer our own question before they get a chance to think. We're trying to help, but in the long run, this extra help does kids a disservice. Children need the experience of forming and using their own common sense, and it's particularly important as children move into the upper grades.

Common sense is about knowing when something is "right." In the story *Goldilocks and the Three Bears,* Goldilocks tried out the food, the beds, and the chairs of the bears. When she came to the right ones, she knew it. How did she know? Being a fairy tale, she "just" knew. But, for our children, living in a real world and not in a fairy tale, knowing when it's just right, or almost just right, is a lot harder.

In this chapter, Randy and Mary don't have Goldilocks's sense of "what's right." Randy needs common sense to keep out of trouble and Mary needs it so that she doesn't get caught up in what other kids think. She needs to believe in what she thinks. Beyond telling our kids to be careful and to use their common sense, what can we do? Telling a child to be careful, which every parent tends to do almost reflexively, is a start, but it's nowhere near enough.

Through the activities and conversations in this chapter:

- **You are helping children gain a deeper sense of what it means to have common sense: to recognize and use good judgment.**
- **You are helping children control their impulsiveness so that they can make more reasoned, common-sense-based decisions.**
- **You are helping children learn how to regulate themselves, to exert self-control when it's needed and to know when it is needed.**

# Staying Out of Trouble

## (Younger Children)

## The Story of Randy

Randy, now in the third grade, is always being told by his teachers, "You ought to know better."

Randy is a good kid, but he always seems to get into trouble. Randy always seems to be getting into or causing accidents . . . not bad accidents but annoying ones . . . even when he is trying to do good.

Today, the girl who sits at the desk next to Randy spilled the grape juice she was drinking. It ran down the front of her dress and onto Randy's desk and onto the floor. It made a purple mess. Randy ran to the sink, got some paper towels and started wiping up the juice that had spilled. Then he knocked over the juice drinks of the two kids sitting on the other side of his desk. Now there were three drinks flowing onto the floor, all over the papers, all over the clothes.

Randy was trying to help but the result was that he made things worse. That happens to Randy a lot. Sometimes he makes things worse by what he says, too. When he saw the purple juice on the kids' clothes, he said: "Boy, you are a real mess!" The teacher came over just then and asked what was happening. The kids replied, "It's all Randy's fault."

That night Randy came home feeling pretty low. He tried to help, and then he got blamed. It was always like that. He always seemed to get into trouble and get blamed. It's not fair. What can he do?

**Reminder:** *Randy gets into a lot of trouble because he tends to act without thinking first or even watching where he is going. He needs to think about what might happen. Spilling the juice is not a really terrible thing, but he makes it worse. Randy needs to understand the importance of being careful, being mindful of what he does even before he does it. He needs to get practice in using his common sense. The responses in this chapter are designed to help children build their own common-sense abilities . . . so that they acquire Goldilocks's ability to know what's right.* ■

## Why Do I Always Get Blamed?

*It might be better if people didn't always have to find someone to blame . . . when things, even little things, go wrong. But there's a natural tendency to want to find out why something bad happens and, yes, to pin the blame on someone.*

*You get blamed because a lot of accidents happen around you. When you went for towels, you did the right thing. When you came back and did not look at how you were cleaning, you were not being careful. And that causes you so much extra trouble. If you would just spend a few moments thinking first, you would receive a lot less blame.*

*And you need to be able to think first before you talk. When you were very little, you may have looked at someone who was handicapped and you pointed and you said something about how that person looked funny. But when you got older, you knew better. As we grow up, we use our common sense to keep our eyes open . . . and sometimes to keep our mouths shut.*

## Why Are the Other Kids Mad at Me?

*Put yourself in their shoes. How would you have felt if the kid next to you had spilt the juice, made your clothes dirty, and then laughed at you?*

---

*I didn't hear you say that you had apologized. You told me that you made some fun of how they looked with the juice all over them. I think you would have been angry if that had happened to you.*

*Think about what you can do now to show that you are sorry and that you will use better judgment from now on.*

**Reminder:** *Remember that just saying "sorry" is not enough. Some kids say they are sorry and do dumb things all over again. They need to spend some time thinking.* ■

## How Can I Keep from Getting into Trouble?

*You probably know the answer to this as well as I do. You need to be more careful. You need to think before you leap. You need to try to see in advance what will happen if you do this or that. That's part of common sense.*

*You need to use your brain to figure things out. When you rushed back with the towels, you needed to look and be observant. You needed to ask yourself, Who else has juice? Will I bump into them?*

*We have to think about how our actions affect the people around us. We have to try to think in advance. It's not easy and sometimes it takes a bad experience to teach us this.*

*We need to see ourselves doing things . . . and doing them well. You have learned something from what happened with the juice. I think you will be more careful from now on.*

## Am I a Bad Kid?

*No, I know that you want to do the right thing, but somehow it doesn't always work out that way. I can see how your teacher and your classmates would get upset with you and start thinking that you aren't such a good kid. You will need to make sure that they know you feel sorry and that you apologized because you felt bad. You will need to let them know that you are going to try to be more careful.*

*When you show them that you care about them, it will make a big difference. But, it can't be something you do for one day or for one week, you really have to keep at it.*

> **Reminder:** *Many children, given the chance, may already know the answers to the questions raised by Randy in this chapter. As parents, we may do more good by listening and nodding rather than by actually telling or advising. When we let our children talk it out, they can come up with some of the best answers.* ■

## *Talking Together: Common Sense—Who's Got It?*

Here's a chance to give a common-sense coaching to others. It's always easier to give advice. Read these examples aloud with your children.

There is a long line at the supermarket. Joey is with his mom . . . and he doesn't feel like waiting. The line looks like it will last forever. His mom has filled the shopping cart. It has taken her over forty-five minutes to find all the things the family needs. Joey keeps on saying, "Let's go, Mom. Let's not wait. I want to go home." Joey starts pulling things out of the cart. She says, "Joey, calm down. You just have to learn to wait."

- What do you think of Joey's behavior?
- What do you think of what his mother says to him?
- What would you say and do if you were Joey's mom or dad?

Barbara sees advertisements for different kinds of dolls and toys on TV. She gets really excited about them. Almost every day she turns to her parents and says, "I just *have* to have that! If you don't get it for me, it means that you don't love me." This makes her parents very upset. They want to show how much they love her, so they give in a lot and buy a lot of these toys.

- Do you think Barbara really needs to have all those toys?
- Do you think Barbara's parents are doing the right thing to buy all those toys?
- Do you know anyone like Barbara?

## Doing Together: Temper, Temper

Anger can look mighty funny in hindsight. By acting out these scenes, we get a picture of ourselves . . . when tempers are cool and common sense comes into play.

Pick any day and act out a time when tempers flared:

- Example: Adults try to put a piece of furniture together using diagrams and it's just not working.
- Example: Children complaining that parents are not fair and they are not getting what they want, etc.

Ask what it looks like and sounds like when:

- Adults get angry
- Children get angry

Now, try the same scenes with a cool head, using good judgment:

- What does it sound like?
- What does it look like?

Think together of a time recently when you each:

- Used your common sense.
- Did not use your common sense.

What would you do differently now in similar situations? In other words, what did you learn?

# I Want to Be Like "Them"

## (Older Children)

## The Story of Mary

Mary travels a long distance to go to a new school across town. She is a very good student. Mary's parents chose this school for her because they heard it offered a strong academic program. Mary went along with her parents' choice even though it meant leaving her own neighborhood and her friends from elementary school.

Mary is doing fine with the schoolwork. But she's not doing fine when it comes to how she feels, especially about how she looks and how she dresses. The kids in her class come from families that have a lot of money.

The other girls seem always to be wearing new clothes from trendy shops. Mary and her parents buy her clothes at the local discount stores. They don't look terrible. But, they don't have the labels the other girls have.

Many days, when Mary gets home from school, she pleads with her parents, "I have to have what the others have. I have to buy my clothes where they do."

One evening, Mary was crying bitterly. That day someone at school laughed at how she dressed. She was more upset than her parents had ever seen: "I'm not as good as the other girls. They will never accept me. If you don't help me and buy me their kind of clothes, I'll just die."

No matter how hard her parents tried to reassure her, they couldn't get through. She seemed so unhappy. What could they do? Finally,

Mary's father suggested that they call his younger sister. She had an experience similar to Mary's. Maybe she could help them.

Mary's aunt urged her parents to listen as much as possible—to let Mary say what she felt without jumping in and cutting her off, to provide a sense of support and balance. Most important, she reminded them, we have to help Mary get a sense of her future, not just of what is happening today.

## You Don't Understand

*Maybe we don't understand everything, but we are trying. We know it's hard for you, in a new school, without your old friends.*

*Your aunt, who grew up in this country, told us how she felt in her new school when she was your age. It helped us to understand what you are going through. She told how the other girls didn't want to make room for her in their group and how she never felt that she was wearing the right clothes. She said that she would be happy to talk with you.*

*We do want you to know that when you feel bad, we feel bad. We want to make it all better, just like when you were a little girl and you fell down at the playground. But we can't. What we can do now is advise you and tell you what we think, and hope you will listen to us. We hope you will talk with us, and we want to keep on talking with you.*

> **Reminder:** *Mary's parents' decision to call her aunt for advice underscores the support system so important to all of us. We don't have to know all the answers in advance, but we do have to try to know where to go to get the help we need. It's not always "experts" who can help. Family and friends are major sources of experience and advice.* ■

## I'll Never Be Accepted

*Sure, you will. First you have to give it some time. Other kids at the school will get to know you, and once they get to know you, you'll have plenty of friends just as you did at your old school.*

*You need time to find the kids at the school who will like you for who you are and not for what you wear.*

*Try to think about why you are at this school and what you want to get from it. It's hard, but try not to think that you have to be like other people. You can be different, you can be yourself . . . and be accepted.*

*You are under pressure to be like everyone else. We know that this happens. But, try not to let one person or incident totally influence you. What you have to do is to try to keep thinking about what's really important and "right" for you. Having fancier clothes is nice. But, most important for you is getting a good education. That's why you are at the new school. That's why you need to make the effort to stay there and get as much out of it as you can.*

> **Stop:** *Share with your child a time when you were in a new situation and you did not feel accepted. Maybe it did not resolve itself with everyone walking hand-in-hand, but you lived through it and so will your child.* ■

> **Reminder:** *Reassurance is not a one-time thing. Count on having to repeat reassurances and check with your child as often as possible about how things are going.* ■

## What Do You Do When You Feel Low?

*Everybody gets low and discouraged sometimes. And everybody has different ways of handling feeling blue.*

*For me, I try to keep remembering the good things that happen and my friends and my family. I count blessings. Yes, it actually helps.*

*Common sense tells us that there will be good days and there will be not-so-good days. Some days you feel like everything is just going to be swell. The sun is shining. The bus came on time. The homework assignment isn't too hard. Your friend called. You get ice cream for dessert.*

*Then there are those other days, when it seems as if so many things are going wrong. The alarm doesn't go off. You are late for school. Your friend is moody. The homework is too hard. The lunch tastes awful.*

*You get the idea. Feelings on any one day fit into a larger picture with many days. On some days, I feel encouraged. On other days, I feel discouraged. That's when I call on my storehouse of good memories. I try to keep focusing on all the good things in my life that I appreciate.*

*From the outside it may not look as if other people have problems, but they do. We all have to try to keep our spirits up, especially when others may not be acting friendly.*

*This does not mean that we have to be mean and make fun of others. It means that we have to keep trying to be our own person.*

## What Does It Mean to Be Your Own Person?

*This is not an easy idea. But let's see if I can explain. There are some people who think they have to be somebody else . . . and not themselves. They think they have to say and think what other people say and think. They really don't make up their own minds and do enough of their own thinking.*

*Usually, it's these same people who have to do what other people do or else they think they won't be accepted. They go to movies they might not even want to see. They wear clothes that might not even look good on them. They eat food that they don't like. They think they have to be "cool" or trendy even when they don't want to be.*

*Being your own person means having a sense of yourself: what you do well, what matters to you. It means to have self-respect. It means to know what's important. That's the balance that common sense helps to give us.*

**Stop:** *Ask your child, "Does this make sense to you? Do you know people who make up their own minds and are their own person?"* ■

## I Worry So Much About School

*We can't argue with you about how you feel. You know better about that than we do.*

*It can help to look at the calendar to try to make a bit of a plan for when things will get better. It might take almost this full school year for you to feel really comfortable at your new school. That might seem like forever, so let's look at it, week by week, month by month.*

*Think about what you can do day by day. Can you go to an after-school club meeting? Can you invite someone to sit with you in the lunchroom? Can you volunteer to help out at a school activity?*

*You need to get to feel more and more at home in your new school. You need to find your own group of friends at school and not worry about who is not letting you into their group.*

*We don't want to forget to mention that you really have to focus on your work. But, just as you make a schedule for your schoolwork, keep on thinking about what you can do to build your life at this new school. Complaining and feeling sorry for yourself is not going to do it, nor will having fancier clothes to wear. This is not easy, but we know that you can do it.*

## Will I Feel Better Soon?

*One day you will think back to this hard time and you will remember the kids in their clothes with the fancy labels, and you may thank them.*

*I am not kidding. We learn important lessons from difficult times. These girls are putting you down and it is forcing you to reach out to find other friends. It is forcing you to think about what you think is important. What you wear on the outside is not really important. It's what you are inside that matters. You know that from us at home and you are learning it at school, too.*

*Not so long ago, kids who were interested in computers got made fun of. Now, those same kids, who kept at their interest in computers, are very important adults in the larger world.*

*You feel bad and we all wish you didn't have to feel bad. But, it's not a catastrophe. You will learn in this experience. You will learn more about being your own person. You will build better judgment and emerge from this with more common sense.*

## Talking Together: Everyone Else Is . . .

It is harder to use common sense when we are under pressure. And children today feel under pressure a lot . . . from TV, from school, from the larger community.

Very often this pressure puts children in the position of being asked to act more grown-up than they really are. Children may not recognize the pressure, but when they feel they need to do what "everyone else" is doing, that's pressure. Children are forever being told that "everyone else is doing it, don't be chicken, be bold, be brave, be cool."

It is important to talk about pressures and how they affect attitudes and behavior. For example:

- Just because your friend has a certain item of clothing, do you need to have it?
- Just because you see other kids shoplifting or breaking a rule, do you feel you have to do it?
- Just because another kid bumps you in the hall, do you feel you have to do something about it?

This is really a version of the old saying, "If someone asks you to jump off a roof, would you do it?" Our children may know better than to do that, but there are many other follow-the-leader temptations they continue to have to deal with, day after day.

We take chances every day but we learn how to try to minimize our risks. For example, the ice on the lake looks thick and hard, but is it? How do we use our common sense? We do it with testing. First, we put our leg out and step gingerly. If the ice makes noise and starts to crack, we jump back to shore. It's more dangerous than we thought. It's not ready for us. That's the kind of step-by-step testing—using common sense—that we can teach our children.

# Doing Together: Using Time Well

For our children to get started on something, we often say, "do one thing at a time." This is sound advice but it's increasingly hard to follow. As children move up through the grades, so much seems to have to get done all at once.

Just as adults need time management help, so do children. They need common-sense practice in organizing their time so that there is time for what has to get done: the school assignments, the extracurriculars, and the free time that kids need for dreaming and growing.

Figuring out how we spend our time helps us know how to change what we're currently doing, even for children. Taking control of our time seems to help us have more time. Parents and children can try this:

- Draw two clock faces or put numbers 1–24 on two ordinary sheets of paper. Use one sheet to draw in times for a typical day. How much time for sleeping? Eating? Work? TV? Homework? Sports? Telephone? etc.
- Ask: Are we spending the right amount of time on the different things that need to be done, things that we care about?
- Use the other clock face to fill in the changes you're recommending for yourselves. Sleeping and eating are necessities, but TV watching may go down and book reading may go up.

This activity helps us focus common-sense attention on our time so that we don't just complain—we do something about it!

# The Adult Connection

## Common Sense

### Now, Later, Never

It seems as if we are always running. We wake up running, from home to work or to the grocery store or to a school meeting. It's hard to catch our breath and to really think about how we are spending our time.

We may actually get to thinking that everything we do is equally important. That can drive us almost crazy and put us way out of balance . . . because there usually isn't enough time to do everything. The deadlines, our jobs, our houses, the kids' school, the meetings. It goes on and on. Our roles as parents and providers and spouses can be overwhelming . . . until and unless we take the time and use common sense to figure out what really matters.

*Now, Later, Never* is an easy exercise used in MegaSkills Programs to help restore perspective and balance in our thinking about what is urgent (*now*), not so urgent (*later*), and what can be dropped (*never*).

That means prioritizing what is important and eliminating what isn't.

Sometimes we want so much to do right by our kids that we forget the importance of doing right by ourselves, too. To do a good job with our children, we have to take care of ourselves, and that means taking care of how we use our energies and spend our time. Without guilt, we need to make our own lives more balanced so that we are doing things for ourselves as well as for our children.

That's what *"now, later, never"* is about. It's one answer to the question: "How can I get it more together?"

This exercise may not solve every problem you have . . . but it goes a long way to uncovering the secret of those other people who seem to keep going despite all they have to do.

The secret is *prioritizing*! It enables us to tackle a mountain of responsibilities with less sweat. We can learn how to figure out what has to be done now, what can be postponed, and what can be ignored.

Take two pieces of blank paper. Keep one blank and divide and label the other into three sections: "Now, Later, Never."

On the blank paper, jot down the tasks you have in whatever order they come to mind. This is your "task bank." When you have a number of responsibilities on your list, move to your labeled pieces of paper. On these, you draw from your "task bank" to make decisions about what responsibilities need to be done *now*, what can be done *later*, and what *never* needs to be done.

An interesting thing about the *never* column is that you may put into it responsibilities you've been doing all along. Now you find they just aren't really that critical.

Once your brain starts thinking like this, you may not be able to stop. Is it *now*? Is it *later*? Is it *never*? You know if you must do something today or whether it can wait. This has to do with how you spend time and the value you put on certain activities. These are individual decisions. When we prioritize what is important, we are more in control and less at the mercy of the competing currents of everyday life.

There is no magic formula to prioritizing. We tend to organize in different ways. Some of us do it with lists; others do it with little notes scattered all over the office and the house; and some of us do it in our heads.

Ask family and friends how they prioritize. What you consider important may not be so important to someone else. Even if you may not agree, it's good to know what others think.

And who says you have to do it all? New findings on how we spend time indicate, for example, that fewer hours each day are being spent on housework. This is not just because of the time-saving devices and services such as washers and vacuums. It's because we are learning to ignore the dust, and to take shortcuts that allow us to have more time for what we really want and need to do.

# Reading Together:
# Common Sense

## Books for Younger Children

*Goldilocks and the Three Bears* retold and illustrated by James Marshall. Dial, 1988.
A contemporary retelling with humorous illustrations tell the tale of the girl who makes herself at home while the Bear family is out.

- Why did Goldilocks go into the Bears' house uninvited? How did the Bears feel when they discovered the intruder? What did Goldilocks and the Bears learn from this experience?

*The Three Little Pigs* retold and illustrated by James Marshall. Dial, 1989.
Full-color illustrations add humor to this retelling of the traditional tale of three pigs who confront the wolf who huffs and puffs at their respective front doors.

- Why did the first and second pigs lose their houses? How did the wolf feel when he couldn't fool the third pig?

*Amelia Bedelia* by Peggy Parish. Illustrated by Fritz Siebel, Harper-Collins, 1992.
A literal-minded housekeeper causes a ruckus when she tries to make sense of the instructions left for her.

- Why does Amelia misinterpret her instructions? How could Mrs. Rogers help Amelia?

## Books for Older Children

*Hog Eye* by Susan Meddaugh. Houghton Mifflin, 1995.
A young pig narrates the story of how she outsmarts a wolf who can't read his recipe for pig soup.

- Why did the pig get off the bus to take the shortcut? Why did the wolf try to cover up his inability to read?

*Doctor DeSoto* by William Steig. Farrar, Straus, Giroux, 1982.
Dr. DeSoto, a mouse dentist, copes with the toothaches of various animals except those with a taste for mice—until the day a fox comes to him in pain.

- Why does Dr. DeSoto break his own rule about the animals for whom he cares? Describe how Dr. DeSoto must feel about the fox's actions.

*Shortcut* by Donald Crews. Greenwillow, 1992.
Children take a shortcut home by walking along a railroad track and find danger as a freight train approaches.

- Why wasn't it a good decision to take the shortcut? How did the children feel when they heard the approaching train? What would the adults say if they knew what the children had done?

# Problem Solving

# Families Learning Together

## Five-Step Problem Solving

**N**O MATTER HOW OLD we are, we are always solving problems. They are the stuff of life. Problem solving is not just for grown-ups. Problem solving is both a grown-up thing and a kids' thing at the same time. To be sure, there are certain problems we think of as grown up. But children are not spared, especially these days, from being involved in lots of what used to be adult-only activities. Because our children are not spared problems, we have to find ways to help them know how to solve them.

To be sure, there are all kinds of problems, some much more scary than others . . . life-or-death ones versus the nagging glitches of everyday life . . . such as how to save time getting to work, how to get kids to eat breakfast, how to make the budget work for the month, how to program the video recorder, and so on. Most of us on most days, thankfully, are caught up in everyday kinds of problems that can be solved, if not perfectly, then at least adequately.

Working on problems that lend themselves to solutions offer us a sense of real, personal achievement. It's the beauty and challenge of figuring out a mystery. It's the surge of satisfaction when we can figure out a shortcut to get downtown, find a new recipe the kids will eat, discover a way to cut down on the monthly bills, or get the video recorder to actually record.

Yet sometimes the load of everyday problems gets so heavy, and problems big and little become so mixed together, that it's hard to sort them out.

That's why we have to be alert for the problems that really can be solved and treasure them. We need to work on ourselves so that when someone, including our child, comes to us and says, "I've got a problem," we don't automatically shrink back. While it's unlikely we'll say, "Oh, good, I love problems," we might be able to say, "Tell me about it. Let's try to figure it out."

We need a system inside our heads that enables us to face problems and to try to manage them. That's our inner capacity for problem solving.

There are a number of complex ways to solve problems. In this chapter we use a very basic five-step system that we can put right into our heads. The goal is to be able to use these steps automatically. They light up in our brains almost as soon as we hear a problem.

## Five-Step System for Parents and Children

**One:** *What's the problem?*
**Two:** *What can we do?*
**Three:** *What do we try first?*
**Four:** *How do we know it's working?*
**Five:** *What do we do next?*

By using a system such as this one and giving our children practice with it, we empower them to use it themselves and not to be dependent on having an adult around to handle problems.

A system like this won't work miracles overnight, but it helps give children the framework they need to deal with the experiences they will face later on their own. In this chapter we listen in as two families work with their children to solve problems using the basic five-step system.

Eric comes home from school and tells his parents that his teacher says he has a problem. It's about how he behaves in the classroom . . . It's a problem that was created at home and it can only be solved at home. Together, Eric and his parents work to figure it out and come up with some solutions they will try to put into practice.

Donna comes home from school announcing that she has learned that she has a problem with being too much of a perfectionist. This is a problem created at home, too. Donna and her parents use the five-step method to figure out what they all need to do differently.

As readers, we don't decide on the one right solution or answer for these problems. We go through the problem-solving system with Eric and his parents, and with Donna and her family. We use the "stops" along the way in this chapter to think through our own and our children's responses to choices facing Eric and Donna.

Through the activities and conversations in this chapter:

- You are helping your children see problem solving as a challenge.
- You are giving your children practice in identifying problems, coming up with a variety of solutions, picking those that are better than others, trying them, and checking on their progress.
- You are helping your child practice a problem-solving system that they can build into their own way of thinking.

# Do It for Me

## (Younger Children)

## The Story of Eric

Almost the first words Eric said when he was a baby were: "Do it for me."

And even though he is in first grade, it hasn't changed. He asks for help all the time, even when he doesn't really need it.

At school, when he has work to do, he tells his teacher that it's just too hard . . . even if it's easy. When he gets home, he pleads with his parents to do it for him, or at least with him.

At home, when his parents ask him to do something such as get dressed for school or pick his toys up, he keeps everybody waiting so long that finally someone else does it for him.

His parents think that maybe if they help him this time, Eric will get the idea and see that things are not so hard. Maybe then he will start to do things on his own. Eric's parents have almost gotten used to how he behaves. Much of the time they don't even notice it. They are on automatic: Eric says he needs help so they give Eric help. Otherwise, he just keeps whining.

Eric's behavior is very noticeable, however, at school. Eric is always telling his teachers that the work is too hard, he can't do it, he just won't, and on and on. He expects to get extra help all the time.

Eric brought this behavior from home into the classroom. And while

---

it may be more tolerable at home, it is disruptive to the rest of the class. His teacher tells him over and over that he needs to stop.

The teacher knows that while Eric may learn to quiet down a bit more in class—especially when she keeps reminding him—the real change for his behavior has to happen at home.

That's when she tells Eric that he has a problem. That's when his parents say, Let's try to solve it together step by step.

## Step One: What Is the Problem?

**What information do we have? What more do we need to have?** *Information is vital. It helps give a bigger picture of the whole situation. The problem is not Eric's alone. It's his parents. It's his history. It's what goes on day in and day out at home.*

**What clues do we have? What are the signs and symptoms?** *Eric whines and his parents give in?*

**What other signs are there?** *Does Eric watch a lot of TV? Does he sleep enough? Does he have friends? How much time does he spend with his parents?*

**When did all this start?** *Eric has been doing this since he started to talk. It just seems to be Eric.*

**Why is it a problem now?** *He's doing it at school and it's not appropriate for school.*

**Is there really a bigger problem?** *Is Eric so starved for attention that he uses whining to get it? Has this become such a habit he doesn't know any other way to behave?*

*Knowing more can help us understand, for example, whether Eric is getting enough attention or whether he craves more. It can help us understand the relationship between Eric and his parents. It helps us put ourselves in Eric's place and get a feel for what he is feeling. It helps define the problem.*

---

**Stop:** *Let's identify Eric's real problem. He might have more than one, but pick one to start the step-by-step problem solving.* ■

## Step Two: What Can We Do?

*The problem that Eric and his family decided to work on is how Eric can learn to handle doing more for himself and not have to keep asking for so much attention from others. They talked about the problem as if it were a puzzle to solve. This made it easier to get started.*

*Once Eric and his family identify the problem, they are ready to brainstorm. That's when they come up with lots of ideas. Some of them are better than others. They don't try to choose or reject anything. They brainstorm: This list should be long . . . both silly and serious.*

*Here are some that Eric's parents came up with:*

> *stop helping Eric*
> *learn to say "NO!"*
> *step back and figure out what's going on*
> *show Eric more love so that he won't feel so unsure and insecure*
> *encourage Eric to make his own choices and to act more grown up*
> *give Eric some rewards for being more grown up*
> *stop rewarding him for being a whiner*

*They asked Eric for his ideas and here are some he came up with on his own:*

> *learn a new way to tell my parents what I want*
> *learn to do things by myself*
> *learn how to act more grown up*
> *learn to get attention in other ways*
> *ask my parents to tell me, "Stop whining!"*

*Talking about the problem as if it belongs to someone else and as if it were a puzzle to solve gives everyone a chance to be more focused on finding solutions and not on finding blame.*

**Stop:** *What other ideas do we have? Which of these ideas are better than the others, and which one should Eric and his parents try first?* ■

## Step Three: What Do We Do First?

*Here's where we give consideration to each of the ideas brainstormed, as though we were in a dressing room trying to decide which suit or dress best fits. One way to sort through these ideas is to grade them with pluses and minuses. This helps to separate the good ideas from the not-so-useful ideas.*

*Taking one idea, here is how Eric and his family grade "Eric needs to learn to do new things all by himself."*

**What's Good (Plus) About This Idea?** *It gets Eric in the habit of helping himself. It can start a new pattern of behavior.*

**What's Not Good (Minus) About This Idea?** *Eric will resist and he'll whine more.*

**To make this idea work, what do we have to do?** *Let's find a specific thing Eric can learn to do . . . something he may really want to learn, such as cooking or skating or swimming or using a computer.*

**Stop:** *We need to ask ourselves whether there are other ideas on the list that deserve the plus and minus check-up. Is this idea really worth trying?* ■

## Step Four: We Try the Idea and Ask Whether It's Working

*Eric and his parents decide to try to help Eric learn a new skill so that he will get into the habit of doing more things for himself. Together they choose to teach Eric how to use the computer. The lessons begin, then Eric starts to practice on his own. They listen, look, and ask. They check for more clues. We check for clues.*

**About Eric:**

- *Is he whining as much as before? Is he whining less? Is he perhaps whining about different things?*
- *Is he doing more for himself? If so, what is it that has changed? What is he doing? How is he being recognized for the new things he is doing?*
- *Has nothing changed? Is Eric just doing his same old routine: "Help me! Do it for me!"*

**About Eric at home with his parents:**

- *Are they doing less for Eric?*
- *Are they resisting his pleas more?*
- *What are they doing that they haven't done before? Has nothing changed? Are they in their same old pattern of listening to Eric's whines and then giving in and just doing it?*

**About Eric at school with his teacher:**

- *Is Eric doing more on his own in class?*
- *Is he tackling assignments with fewer pleas for help?*
- *Is he beginning to say: "I can do this!"*

**Stop:** *Think together. How do we know when we are meeting our goals? Do we have to figure out in advance what we want to accomplish and find ways to measure it as we move along? Do we think that Eric will change his behavior for the better?* ■

## Step Five: What Do We Do Next?

*We assess. We decide if our idea is making a difference. If it is, we move forward and keep at it. If it's not, we go back to our brainstorming list and try another idea.*

*In this case Eric finds that he is using the computer on his own, and he is whining less. He now knows more about the computer than his parents. Next step? They have asked him to teach them how to get on the Internet. They are now asking him for help.*

*Not all of Eric's problems are solved. His teacher reports that things are better, but Eric now seeks extra attention by showing off his computer skills. Instead of the old "help me," it's become more of "look at me." But, everyone feels that this is progress. Eric is moving towards a greater sense of his own abilities and his own place in the group. The future is definitely looking brighter.*

> **Reminder:** *Problem solving in real life is not out of the textbook. Breaking down a problem into five steps makes its solutions sound so neat. Problem solving is actually messy. We poke around but in a kind of systematic way. It's a little like what happens when we go to the doctor with a problem and she makes a diagnosis. She might treat it with different medicines until a breakthrough occurs and the treatment shows signs of working. It's after this experimentation that we know that the problem is on the road to being solved.* ■

## Talking Together: Everyday Choices

Do we recognize when we are problem solvers? Children may think that problem solving is something only grown-ups do.

One of the most basic forms of problem solving is making choices. Here's a chance to talk together about the different choices that adults and children make every day. Some examples:

- What to wear to school? Whether to wear the red shirt or blue one.
- What to eat for dessert? Whether to have chocolate cake or ice cream or both.
- How much and which TV shows to watch? Whether to do chores first or watch TV and do chores later . . .

Ask children to select a decision, any one of the many they make each day, and talk together about what went into it. For example, ask them why they watch certain TV shows? Try to help children explain more than "I just like it." Ask children *why?* Encourage them to give at least one reason.

> **Reminder:** *Share with your child a decision you had to make recently and be sure to talk about how you made the decision. It does not have to be a momentous one. For example: How do you decide what brands of food to buy at the supermarket? What goes into your decision? Price? Quality? Convenience? When you share your thinking, children see your model of decision making.*
>
> *They need to be aware about how much problem solving they do everyday in their own ways. The more practice children get in making their own decisions and learning to live with the consequences of their decisions, the stronger and more confident they become as problem solvers.* ∎


## *Doing Together: Looking In on Others*

Discuss the scenes below and talk about the choices made by these parents and children. Then try acting them out. It's fun and revealing . . . to see what those *others* do and, maybe, what *we* do

Sara always seems to take longer to do things than anybody else. She takes forever to get out of bed. Then, she takes forever to get dressed. Her parents have to check on her over and over and ask, "Are you ready yet, Sara?" When she is asked to pick up her toys, she whines and she waits until her parents get really angry. They ask: "What's wrong with you, Sara? Why do you do this?"

Then Sara says, "I'm sorry. I won't do it again." The next day she does it all over again.

- What do you think is wrong with Sara?
- Do you know anyone like Sara?
- What do you think her parents should say and do?

Brian does things very fast. He finishes his work before the other students. When he's done, he gets up from his seat and starts walking around the room. He bothers the other kids. He leans over their desks picking up papers and making noises at the pencil sharpener. He doesn't realize it, but he's making it hard for other children to concentrate. Brian wonders why the other kids don't like him.

- What do you think?
- What advice do you want to give Brian?
- What do you think the teacher ought to do?

**Reminder:** *Play is often more instructive than lecture. When children act out a scene, or visualize it, they get a better sense of what to expect from themselves and from others.* ■

# The Perfectionist Trap

## (Older Children)

## The Story of Donna

Donna is a perfectionist. She worries over every little thing. Her bed has to be made just so. Her clothes are always hung up just so, and everything on her desk is just so. Donna's been like this a long time. In the early grades in school, her perfectionism helped her. Her teachers said that she never got anything wrong. And her parents praised her.

Donna is the oldest child in the family, the one who has been responsible, careful, thorough, and grown up from the start. Her parents now realize that Donna was always expected to be "grown up," to do things right from the start.

But as Donna has grown older, her perfectionism has become less helpful. In fact, it's an obstacle. Now that she's in the upper grades, Donna's assignments have become more difficult. It's expected that even good students will make mistakes as they try out different ways to work through problems. But when Donna does make a mistake, it is a blow to her. One mistake, such as a grammar or spelling error, and she starts generalizing about how she can't do anything right.

Instead of gaining interest in her schoolwork as it becomes more complex and challenging, she's losing interest because she's so worried all the time. Her teacher is becoming increasingly concerned and has told Donna that this is a problem that she has to work on.

For Donna to succeed as a student in school and later on in life, she has to be able to take the risks it takes to learn new subjects, to stumble, to get up, and to keep going. She needs to be able to make mistakes and learn from them. She needs to be able to learn how to cope with disappointment.

Donna's teacher understands how over-perfectionism can hurt and not help. Donna and her parents can now work on the problem. We follow them as they use the five-step problem-solving method.

## Step One: What's the Problem?

*It is true that you do have more work to do now that you are in the upper grades. But it is also true that you are much too hard on yourself. This is making it difficult for you to do your best.*

*Everyone makes mistakes. This means parents, teachers, classmates, and the best athletes and scholars in the world. We have to learn to accept that we cannot be perfect.*

*Making mistakes is not the problem. The problem is in how we handle our mistakes. We can either say to ourselves, "Well, that didn't work. I have to try something different next time." Or, we can get down on ourselves and say, "I never do anything right."*

*You don't have to be perfect for us to love you and for you to like yourself. We expect you to try your best, but we also expect you to make honest mistakes.*

*Sometimes good things actually happen when we make mistakes. We learn what we have to do differently. We learn about new paths to take. And sometimes mistakes turn out to be real breakthroughs. Penicillin, one of the first antibiotics that has saved many, many lives, was discovered after the scientists made what they thought was a mistake.*

*Maybe we have gotten you too worried about doing things wrong. Maybe we got too upset when you spilled the milk or didn't bring home the top grades in the class. Maybe that gave you the idea that you just had to do everything right, or else. Maybe that's what made you think that you have to be perfect. If you got that idea from us, then that's a mistake that we've made. Parents make plenty of mistakes. There are no instructions that come with a baby. Most of all, we have to think about the future, about what we will try to do differently next time. Like skaters in a big race who fall down and get right back up, that's what we have to do when we make mistakes.*

**Stop:** *What do you think about what Donna's parents say? Have you ever had a problem similar to Donna's?* ∎

## Step Two: What Can I Do?

*You do have more work to do than before. That's true. And you will be able to do it, maybe not all perfectly, but very well. When we stop worrying about being perfect, it's easier to do our work. When we worry about making a mistake, we get tense and we tend to make more of them. Our hands become clumsier, our brain doesn't think as well, we get tongue tied.*

*It sounds like a silly thing to say, but you need more experience with mistakes and getting over them. We don't want you to become careless and sloppy, but it wouldn't hurt to relax a bit.*

*Let's think about things each of us can do. This calls for brainstorming.*

### Donna's Ideas

*don't worry so much*
*take up a hobby*
*forgive myself in advance*
*concentrate more*
*pay attention*

### Her Parents' Ideas

*ease up on Donna*
*encourage Donna to ease up on herself*
*learn to respond to mistakes in a different way*
*talk about mistakes that others make*
*help Donna understand what's going on*

**Stop:** *Which of these ideas do you think has the most chance to help Donna? Which would you pick if you were Donna and her parents? Any other ideas to share?* ■

**Reminder:** *Keep teachers informed about actions being taken at home to help solve children's problems. Teachers will add their own ways to help in the classroom. Teachers help students like Donna by teaching them how to tackle assignments, how to feel more at ease in the classroom and that it's OK to make a mistake and to learn from it.* ■

## Step Three: What Do I Do First?

*Together pick one assignment and start. Say aloud in advance, "I will do my best and try very hard not to worry about having to make it perfect."*

*Because book reports, papers, and creative writing can cause a lot of anxiety, start with those.*

- *Take a blank piece of paper and scribble at least ten words on it—any words, any words at all. This gets rid of the dread of putting the first words on the totally clean sheet of paper. Parents and children can do this together.*
- *Now, either using that sheet or another cleaner one, your child brainstorms ideas for the paper. Assume a topic is assigned, anything from A to Z—pick something. Come up with ideas, any thoughts, in any order.*
- *Next, your child goes down this list of ideas, putting numbers next to each. What comes first? second? third? etc. This sketches out an orderly sequence.*
- *Now your child is ready to write, using the ideas in the order of the numbers.*
- *Encourage your child to write fast, without editing the first draft. Then read the draft over, cut, add, make some changes. Now you have a legible, revised final draft to be handed in.*

*This process may not result in the greatest essay in the world, but it does result in an essay. That's important for cutting through excessive worrying. PS: It really works!*

**Stop:** *We all have our own ways to get started on assignments that seem daunting. Some people talk to themselves, giving themselves a pep talk. Others pile books in the middle of the room so there is no way to avoid the task. Any special first steps to share?* ■

## Step Four: How Do I Know When It's Working?

*You know when it's working when you hear yourself say or feel:*

- *"OK: it's not the end of the world."*
- *"What can I learn from this? Did I learn another way to handle the situation?"*
- *"Next time I'll ask for help when I don't understand something."*
- *"I am not expected to know everything in advance. What I am expected to do is to try to learn from my mistakes."*
- *"I am not so scared anymore."*

*If it's not working, you change course. You come up with an alternative way to deal with the problem. The topic you pick for your paper just doesn't work out, so you pick another one. The cake you baked tastes awful so you decide to choose another recipe next time. The model airplane you put together doesn't fly so you try another model. We have to keep going, no matter what.*

**Stop:** *Talk together about a mistake you have made recently and what you learned as a result of making it. Also share the near-miss: the mistake that almost was and how you avoided it. It's those old mistakes that often help us avoid the future ones.* ■

## Step Five: What Do I Do Next?

*It's good to see you getting more and more comfortable with yourself as a person who can make a mistake and keep on going: like the violinist who strikes a wrong note and keeps on playing, like the ball player who misses a catch and still finishes the game, like the scientist whose experiment didn't work out and who goes onto the next one . . .*

> **Reminder:** *We are all scientists, with or without degrees. We make hypotheses, we test them each day, and we test again. We try to learn a little more each day, and use this new learning in new ways. It's the wonder—the joy and pain—of being human.* ■

## Talking Together: Pictures Worth Many Words

Together with your child, select pictures from newspapers or magazines that illustrate problems. These can be natural or human disasters, or they can represent a variety of positive experiences such as children marching in a parade or new animals at the zoo or candidates declaring their election win. Before sharing them, cut off the captions beneath the pictures.

The goal is to guess the problem (or to make up one) and come up with as many solutions as possible for the people or events in that picture.

For example: Does your picture show a flood? An accident? A group of people at a meeting? Guess:

What is the problem that needs to be solved?
What solutions can be tried?
Which ones do you think will be selected and why?
How will they know what's working?

Do the same with TV programs. Cut off the sound. Look at the picture and try to guess the story line. Or, retaining the sound and hearing the plot, think of other ways the story could have ended. When children do this, they are both the problem makers and problem solvers.

You may not have to "make up" a problem. There's probably one at home just waiting to be solved. Pick one and start the five-step system. Big or little, new or old, focus on it with the problem-solving model and see what headway you can make.

## Doing Together: Making Changes

To solve problems usually requires change. It's much easier for children to make change than it is for adults. We get entrenched in our way of doing things and need drastic action to move out of comfortable habits.

But even for adults, change, like journeys, start with a single step. In this activity we start right at home, in our own bedrooms and living rooms.

Talk together about personal habits. Little ones or big ones . . . they are hard to change. For the sake of practice, see if you can recognize at least one thing that you do habitually. Then, try to change it for the sake of practice.

For children:

- Which sock do you usually put on first?
- Which side of the bed do you sleep on?
- Do you wash your face first or brush your teeth?

For adults:

- Which light do you put on first in the morning and put out last at night?
- When you read the newspaper, what section do you read first?
- When you watch TV, what channel do you turn to first?
- When you start to clear up a room, what do you clear first?

These are not big changes we are talking about. They are small, but they illustrate that when we get into habits, we usually keep on doing the same thing over and over.

The same is true for bigger changes. When we acquire practice in changing habits, we have a better chance of being able to make the changes needed to solve larger problems.

We get a great feeling when we tackle a problem and figure out some ways to try to solve it. That's a lift in itself. When we actually solve it, there is almost no better feeling in the whole world. Problems can cause pain, yes—but they also carry within them the potential for great joy.

# The Adult Connection

## Problem Solving

## *The Benefits of Experience*

As we grow older, what we accumulate (besides extra pounds) are years and experiences. There's no way to go backward on the years. The only choice we have is to use our experiences and make them count for us.

Big experiences stay in our memory. The little ones, those small, unremarkable moments that make up our daily lives, tend to get overlooked. We solve them or we don't solve them, but we have to deal with them.

From the still broken lawn mower that we thought we fixed, to the term paper that didn't get a high grade, to the job promotion that didn't come through, to the child who argues that we're rotten parents—all these experiences become part of the experience bank. Even bad experiences aren't wasted. It's how we use them that matters.

How do we reap the most benefit from all this experience? Here are three tips that I've found helpful:

**Observe Everyday Experiences.**   Notice the small things and enjoy as many as possible. When things go wrong or mistakes are made, try to maintain your sense of balance and proportion as you respond and react.

There are experiences that move us along and those that bog us down. We need to recognize the difference between them. We have to try to

---

recognize when things are getting better and when we have done all that we can. That's the wisdom we struggle to achieve.

**Keep on Track.** The attic room needs cleaning. Files need to be set up. Three guests are coming for dinner. There's an unexpected assignment on the job.

Everything clamors to be done at once. So, we force ourselves to plan and to ask: "What do I tackle first, second, third?" And pretty soon, things start getting done, not necessarily in the order other people would do them, but in an order that makes sense for us.

### Ask, "How Am I Doing?"

Am I putting my experience to work for me or am I sweating hard but going in the wrong direction?

In what ways am I working too hard? What's coming easily to me? Am I using my strengths to help overcome my weaker areas?

Do I forgive myself when things are not going well? Do I make changes needed as quickly as I can?

Do I try to take pride in a job that turned out well and pause . . . even for a moment or two to recognize my success?

Do I let my children see me enjoying our life together?

We may not be able to answer *yes* to each of these questions all of the time . . . but a *yes* now and then is mighty important.

## Still a Lot to Solve

We wouldn't have to worry about obstacles and problems in learning if we already knew everything we needed to know.

The reality is that we still have a lot to learn. A prestigious university recently asked its faculty to come up with questions that still need answering. They identified an "agenda of ignorance" for the next generation which includes:

- How we learn and how our memories work
- How genes and viruses work and what to do about cancer
- How to predict the weather and do something about it

- How to plan a safe mission to Mars
- How national economies grow and how to make businesses successful
- How to work with the changes brought by worldwide electronic communications

To solve these and other questions will take children (and adults—it's not too late for us) who are fearless problem solvers. We need to be ready to make mistakes, learn from them, and move on to the new questions that are sure to follow.

# Reading Together:
# Problem Solving

## Books for Younger Children

*Caps for Sale* by Esphyr Slobodkina. W. R. Scott, 1947.
A peddler must figure out how to retrieve his caps after they are stolen by a band of mischievous monkeys.

- How did the peddler react when he first discovered his caps missing? What strategies did he use to get them back?

*The Doorbell Rang* by Pat Hutchins. Greenwillow, 1986.
Guests begin to arrive soon after the cookies are out of the oven.

- How does the family resolve the dilemma of making certain each guest gets a cookie? How do the children feel sharing their cookies?

*Sara and the Door* by Virginia Jensen. Illustrated by Ann Strugnell. Addison-Wesley, 1977.
While trying to free herself from the front door, Sara learns about buttons; she gets out by unbuttoning her coat!

- What was Sara's initial reaction to being caught in the door? Why did it take her so long to figure how to get out of the situation?

## Books for Older Children

*Chattanooga Sludge* by Molly Bang. Harcourt Brace, 1996.
John Todd attempts to clean the toxic waters of the Chattanooga Creek by creating a Living Machine. This story is based on actual events and people.

 • What characteristics did Todd demonstrate while pursuing answers to the dilemma? How did he refine his methodology?

*Sam and the Tigers* by Julius Lester. Illustrated by Jerry Pinkney. Dial, 1996.
A boy named Sam matches wits with tigers who want to eat him.

 • How effective are the strategies used by the tigers? How does Sam's family help him solve his problem?

*Who's in Rabbit's House?* by Verna Aardema. Illustrated by Leo & Diane Dillon. Dial, 1977.
Rabbit has a problem: Someone is inside her house and will not let her in! This well-told African folktale is illustrated to look like a village play.

 • How does Rabbit respond to all of the advice she is given? How can the smallest of all the animals solve Rabbit's problem?

# Growing Along
# with Our Children

**Y**OU CAN PICK THEM out in the crowd: the parents who seem to be doing their parenting almost naturally and the ones who, while trying hard, are struggling. It shows, and it shows on the children, too.

At the local public library, I observed a tall father and his small son. They would have been hard to avoid anyway. All the time they were in the library, the little boy, about three, was talking very loudly, pushing books and audio tapes around. It was a real pay-attention-to-me routine. The father, to his credit, kept on repeating, "We have to be quiet. Shhh."

The words were fine, but his face said something else to his son and to anyone watching. His face said, "Isn't this boy of mine something? Isn't he smart? Isn't he terrific?" The son saw this message, so he kept on talking and laughing. His pay-attention-to-me behavior was getting his father's approval, despite the words he mouthed.

When last seen, the father was carrying his son on his shoulders as he moved about the library and the boy was laughing and talking at the top of his lungs. This got the child away from the bookshelves. But, it sent a mixed message to the boy: Be quiet and be playful and noisy at the same time. It's no wonder that children can get confused.

The same day I saw another family at the swimming pool: mother, dad, and two young children. The kids were boisterous, but not overly so. Their parents repeated, "There are others here: Don't splash." The children listened. And they did not splash.

But something else very important was going on. The parents were making sure that their children were learning how to swim. They provided messages of encouragement and actions that put across the message. Mom and Dad, moving a few feet away from the kids, urged, "Swim to us." When the little one said, "No, I can't," they said, "Let's do it together." And they did.

Each time, the parents swam a bit farther. Each time they encouraged their children to swim and reinforced their success. The children were not showing off; they were showing they could do it. And so were their parents! Their messages were clear and direct and followed by appropriate actions.

We don't start out knowing how to be good parents. This learning is lifelong. While it would be a lot easier to learn when our children are young, thank goodness it's really never too late. We are lucky. As we live longer, we have an opportunity to keep learning longer. Basically that means we keep growing up.

When psychologists tell us what it takes to be a grown-up, they usually talk about maturity and relationships. As an educator, I think about learning and what it takes to keep on learning. I recently learned to change a tire. While it hurt a bit more bending over than it would had I learned this in my teens or twenties, it was a lesson I could still learn.

And, I got a chance in this simple, everyday activity to practice MegaSkills: among them **Confidence** (I could do it); **Motivation** (willingness to learn); **Teamwork** (someone taught me to do it); **Common Sense** (I need to know this); and **Caring** (when I do this myself, I don't have to get someone else out of bed in the middle of the night).

These very characteristics we encourage in our children to help them do well in school apply to us as grown-ups. But they apply in a different way—not to prepare for some far-off future but to help live productively in the present.

It's great to know that we live long enough these days to have a chance to learn MegaSkills again, even if we did not learn them so well as children. True, some of us came by our parenting skills quite naturally. For the rest of us, we work on them. I am still working on them, and some days are better than others.

To be the best parent we can be takes practice. And it's not gained easily. This book has been about getting practice in what we can say and what we can do to build our children's abilities to achieve and to tackle the everyday problems that come home from school.

If along the way we have built our own abilities as adults, it's not an accident. We grow right along with our children. It's a truly remarkable opportunity and it's here for all of us.

# Acknowledgments

*What Do We Say? What Do We Do?* owes a lot to family, colleagues, and organizations who helped me know What to Say and What to Do over many years:

To Spencer Rich, my husband, whose confidence in me gives me confidence.

To our daughters, Rebecca and Jessica and her husband Jon, who use their MegaSkills® as they keep reminding me of what to say and do as a parent.

To my parents, Hyman and Rose Kovitz, whose MegaSkilled advice still rings in my ears.

To the remarkable group of colleagues supporting the Home and School Institute: To the Board and Advisers of the Institute, who over the years have stalwartly given advice and provided the moral support it has taken to enable the Institute to survive and to grow. Special thanks to the Institute's treasurer, Jim Van Dien, for his effort and perseverance. And to Mickey Bazelon, Chair of the Institute's National Advisory Council, for her caring and motivation.

To Harriett Stonehill, Director of the MegaSkills Education Center, who has been the driving force in establishing the MegaSkills workshop program and who is spearheading the launch of the What Do We Say? What Do We Do?® parent discussion groups nationally.

To Beverly Mattox, Senior Consultant to HSI, and the team of Field Associates and Site Coordinators, among them, Judy Brim, Tom Catlett,

Gwen Dixon-Coe, Tonie Fuentes, Karen Geiger, Cynthia Geraghty, Brenda Kennedy-Snyder, Jackie La Bouff, and Mo Sanders, who, working with others, ensure high quality Institute services in communities, large and small, across our great nation.

To Kathleen Doherty of Tor Books for her wise counsel and to her colleagues who have made this book possible; to Susan Leon for her thoughtful comments on the manuscript, to Judy Abbate for her fine graphics, to Nicole Slanco of Tor for getting the parts together, and to Harold Roth, my agent and friend, for bringing us all together.

To Maria Salvadore, Children's Services Coordinator of the District of Columbia Library, for her invaluable work on the Reading Together sections.

To Rachel Z. Ayala, Outreach Coordinator of HSI, who makes sure that the Institute reaches out and responds to communities nationally, to Joan Worden, for her continuing counsel, and to Rachel Venzant, who has deciphered this manuscript with great care.

To the national organizations the Institute works with closely, among them: American Library Association, National Education Association, National Association of Elementary School Principals, Council of the Great City Schools, National Association of Federal Education Program Administrators, Phi Delta Kappa, National Alliance of Business.

To the more than 11,000 MegaSkills leaders who, from all walks of life, have come ready and committed to helping others. This is a diverse group, from across the nation . . . parents, grandparents, teachers, business people, working in a variety of settings from schools to workplaces to housing centers and hospitals. And to the next generation of leaders of the What Do We Say? What Do We Do? discussion programs, extending the impact of MegaSkills.

The numbers of us ready to help educate families and children are good signs in times when some say we just don't care about each other anymore. The truth is—we do.

# Index

# About the Author

Dorothy Rich, Ed.D., called the "Dr. Spock of Education," is founder and president of the nonprofit Home and School Institute (HSI) based in Washington, DC. Recognized internationally for her expertise in family educational involvement, she is the author of the original *MegaSkills* and the developer of the MegaSkills training programs. The focus of her work is on helping families and educators team together to build achievement for children and adults.

Dr. Rich's work has received the A+ for Breaking the Mold Award from the U.S. Department of Education and support from the MacArthur Foundation among others. Dr. Rich's work has been found to be effective in raising student achievement, decreasing discipline problems and TV watching time, and increasing homework time. School districts contract with the Home and School Institute to bring MegaSkills training and resources to their communities. Dr. Rich's work has been featured in the *Washington Post, The New York Times, The Los Angeles Times,* NBC's "Today" show, *Education Week,* "Good Morning America," and *Reader's Digest.*

Among Dr. Rich's newest resources now available to families, schools, businesses, and nonprofit organizations are *The Power of MegaSkills* (Houghton Mifflin, 1997) and *What Do We Say? What Do We Do?* (Forge, 1997). Dr. Rich invites readers to contact her at the Institute to learn more about these and related Institute programs:

The MegaSkills Education Center
Home and School Institute
1500 Massachusetts Ave. NW
Washington, DC 20005

202-466-3633
http://www.MegaSkillsHSI.org

# *If You Like* What Do We Say? What Do We Do?

## *You'll Want to Know More About Home and School Institute Programs and Services . . .*

The Home and School Institute (HSI) is an independent, nonprofit educational organization. Since 1972, HSI, founded by Dr. Dorothy Rich, develops programs to support the educational role of the family and the role of schools in teaming with families and communities. HSI designs and implements partnerships among the complex forces that play a role in educational improvement today.

## *MegaSkills Training Programs*

**MegaSkills Leader Training Workshops:**  The MegaSkills Education Center trains and certifies MegaSkills leaders to conduct parent workshops. This program, now in 48 states (and also available in Spanish), is sponsored by schools, businesses, and community organizations.

**MegaSkills Essentials for the Classroom:**  This program trains teachers/leaders to provide MegaSkills activities for schools and organizations, in character-development and MegaSkills attitudes and behaviors.

**MegaSkills Schools:**   This is the newest HSI program designed to expand the impact of MegaSkills. MegaSkills Schools combines three synergistic components: classroom curriculum, parent workshops, and the MegaSkills environment.

To learn more about these acclaimed training institutes, sponsored by schools and businesses, check the MegaSkills web page: http://www.MegaSkillsHSI.org Fax: 202-833-1400 or call 202-466-3633.

## *MegaSkills-Related Publications*

**Discussion Guides for *What Do We Say? What Do We Do?*:**   Ideal for PTAs and parent meetings, these guides, available in quantity from HSI, use this book as the base for self-study and discussion groups in schools and libraries across the nation.

The HSI Parent Shelf Library contains a variety of parent education books, including *MegaSkills*, published by Houghton Mifflin, and *What Do We Say? What Do We Do?*, published by Forge. Book orders from the HSI office require a minimum, prepaid order. For a copy of the HSI publication list and a free MegaSkills Message, "Vacation Education," send a stamped, self-addressed envelope to: The Home and School Institute, MegaSkills Education Center, 1500 Massachusetts Avenue, NW, Washington, DC 20005.